ALMAH — VIRGIN OR YOUNG WOMAN?

by

George L. Lawlor, Th.D.

Professor of Greek and Bible
Cedarville College
Cedarville, Ohio 45314

Published by
Regular Baptist Press
1800 Oakton Boulevard
Des Plaines, Illinois 60018

Library of Congress catalogue card number 73-76072

Printed in the United States of America

Contents

Foreword

The Virgin Birth of Christ is a *sine qua non* of our holy Christian faith. It is a cardinal doctrine and one of the fundamentals of our belief. Without it true Christianity does not exist. It is, then, one of the exalted themes for our contemplation of Christ. It is the heart of God's intervention in the realm of Satan by the advent of our Lord.

From this basic tenet of our faith there flows the whole stream of redemptive truth wherein rests man's only hope. To deny the Virgin Birth of Christ is to not be a Christian in the Biblical sense.

Dr. George L. Lawlor has ably presented the Scriptural teaching on this subject. In so doing he has uncovered the unbelief of false teachers who are in reality "blind leaders of the blind" and "wolves in sheep's clothing." He also brings to light the error in this area of some of the modern Bible Versions of our day.

We welcome this volume as a valuable addition to the bibliography on Christology and predict for it a fruitful ministry of the printed page.

JOSEPH M. STOWELL, D.D.
NATIONAL REPRESENTATIVE OF
THE GENERAL ASSOCIATION OF
REGULAR BAPTIST CHURCHES

5

Introduction

The attitude of liberal theology toward the Doctrine of Christ is clearly evident in the two widely popular editions of the Bible—the Revised Standard Version, sponsored by the National Council of Churches, and the New English Bible. The latter was produced under the direction of a joint committee representing the leading protestant denominations, British and Foreign Bible Society, and the National Bible Society of Scotland. The Revised Standard Version New Testament was published in 1946, and the final publication of the entire Bible took place in 1952. In 1970, the complete New English Bible was published, and has taken its place along with the Revised Standard Version.

In these versions there have been some improvements in literary style, and a number of changes affecting words and phrases which are helpful. But there are many needless changes, conjectures, obscurations, inconsistencies, inaccuracies, and new readings in the Revised Standard Version and the New English Bible. These reveal the theological bias of the revisers and translators, and constitute a definite attack upon the great eternal verities of the Holy Scriptures. This critical assault is directed particularly against the Doctrine of Christ, the focal point of which is the Virgin Birth of our Lord Jesus Christ. The move against the Doctrine of the Virgin Birth of Christ is clearly set forth by the deliberate mistranslation of the key Hebrew word *almah* in the crucial passage in Isaiah 7:14.

The KJV[1] text in Isaiah 7:14, in the second clause, reads: "Behold, a *virgin*[2] shall conceive, and bear a son, and shall call his name Immanuel." The RSV and the NEB remove the word *virgin* from this great verse and translate: "Behold, a *young woman* shall conceive, and bear a son, and shall call his name Immanuel." The word *virgin* is then placed below the text proper in a small footnote, as a secondary alternate reading. Hence the revisers clearly reveal their own attitude toward the doctrine of the Virgin Birth of Christ, and raise a serious question concerning any reference to the Virgin Birth of Christ in this prophecy. This leaves many in a state of confusion and indecision. If indeed the translators truly believed the doctrine of the Virgin Birth of Christ, and if the word *virgin* is in truth a correct rendering of the Hebrew term used, then certainly there is no valid reason for removing the word *virgin* from the verse.

1 "KJV" is an abbreviation for *King James Version*. "RSV" and "NEB" are abbreviations for *Revised Standard Version* and *New English Bible*, and are so used throughout the remainder of this book.

2 Italics in Scripture texts are used by the author for emphasis throughout the remainder of this book.

The theological mind and position of the translators are thus clearly revealed. The word "virgin" (Hebrew *almah*) occurs nine times in the Old Testament. In four of these occurrences, these men have translated it "maiden" or "maidens" (Ps. 68:25; Prov. 30:19; Song of Sol. 1:3 and 6:8). But in Isaiah 7:14, they have not only rejected the word "virgin," but they have declined to use the word "maiden," which they use to translate the Hebrew word *almah* in the other four texts. Dr. Alva J. McClain has aptly commented:

> Why was the great prophecy of Isaiah 7:14 selected as a place where neither *virgin* nor *maiden* would be allowed, but instead they translate *a young woman?* Does this not provide very clear evidence that in the thinking of these revisers the *young woman* in question was not a *virgin?*[1]

The liberal scholars and ecumenical churchmen have thus revealed their definite theological bias toward the Doctrine of Christ—the Doctrine of the Virgin Birth in particular. In answer to their critical attack, it is the purpose of this book to show that the Doctrine of the Virgin Birth of Christ is an indispensable fundamental of the true faith. The meaning of the Hebrew word *almah* in the great key prophecy of Isaiah 7:14 is crucial. The evidence for its proper meaning of "virgin," which the true Christian Church has staunchly maintained through the generations of history, is substantial.

---

1 Dr. Alva J. McClain, "The Virgin Birth in the RSV," *The Brethren Missionary Herald*, (February 28, 1953), p. 138.

The passages in which the word *almah* occurs are the following.

Genesis 24:43   Proverbs 30:19
Exodus 2:8   Song of Solomon 1:3; 6:8
1 Chronicles 15:20   Isaiah 7:14
Psalms 46:1; 68:25

An examination of these passages of Scripture, most particularly the great prophetic announcement in Isaiah 7:14, will clarify the sense and significance of the word *almah,* and will expose the heretical and indefensible character of the RSV and NEB translations. They should be condemned without hesitation by all true believers because of their grammatical inaccuracy, and not less importantly on account of their moral and theological implications.

Part One

Part One

I

An Examination of the Use of Almah in the First Eight of the Nine Old Testament Passages

1. THE USE OF *almah* IN GENESIS 24:43.

There can be no doubt as to the meaning of *almah* in this verse. It characterizes Rebekah, to whom verse 16 refers as "a virgin, neither had any man known her...." It is true that the word "virgin" in verse 16 is not *almah*, but *bethulah*, a more familiar word for "virgin," which however describes a maiden who has been secluded from intercourse with men, derived from the verb *bathal*, "to seclude, separate, keep in privacy" (Deut. 22:23, 28). The word *almah* denotes a lass or young maiden who has been kept in private, out of sight, veiled and reserved from carnal contacts and relationships, and who is about to emerge from her sheltered young life in contemplation of marriage. But both terms are used of Rebekah, which leaves no question as to the meaning intended.

In answer to those who object that the words *almah* and *bethulah* themselves do not prove that Rebekah was a virgin, it should be noted: (1) that the two words do testify to the meaning of "virgin" as their usage shows, and (2) that the usual words for a young female are used in verse 8, "woman" (Hebrew, *ish-shah*), and in verse 14, "damsel" (Hebrew, *nah-arah*). When the writer wished to designate *the kind* of young woman God had chosen as a wife for Isaac, the Holy Spirit constrained him to use both *almah* and *bethulah*. The word *bethulah* is indeed the more customary term to designate a "virgin," but it is not a more definite word. Either word would have been sufficient to describe the character of Rebekah, but the use of both words is emphatically conclusive, and *almah* is sharply determinative. In addition to this, all possible lingering doubt is dispelled by the clause in verse 16, "neither had any man *known* her." The verb "known" is the Hebrew *yadah*—the term found in Genesis 4:1, "And Adam *knew* [*yadah*] Eve, his wife, and she conceived and bore Cain." The verb "knew" has reference to connubial intercourse; hence the statement that no man *had known* Rebekah significantly stresses the fact of her virginal purity.

2. THE USE OF *almah* IN EXODUS 2:8.

Almah is translated "maid" in the KJV rendering of this verse, descriptive of Miriam, the sister of the infant Moses. She had probably been sent by Moses' mother to watch the proceedings after Moses had been placed in the ark of bulrushes at the riverside. No doubt all had been prepared beforehand by the mother who had selected the place and time for Moses to be found, from a knowledge of the character and habits of the daughter of Pharaoh, and so far as it was possible had instructed her what to do and say. From the brief narrative in Exodus 2:1-8, it appears that Miriam carried out the instructions given her with surprising tact, resourcefulness, and courage. She later became an envious woman and aspired for equality with her brother Moses, speaking out against him and his leadership. However at the beginning, at this point of time, she was the young maiden watching over the life of her infant brother in the providence of God.

The conduct of Miriam as the watcher over her infant brother Moses makes possible the fair assumption that she was between ten and fifteen years old when Moses was born. This fact means that she was approximately 140 years old when she died (Num. 20:1). There is no reason to assume that she was more than fifteen years of age, despite the use of the Greek "neanis" for *almah* in the Septuagint version. The word "neanis" has a rather wide range of usage, and is occasionally used in Greek writings to describe a young man or woman of more than twenty years of age (as in Acts 7:58; Titus 2:4). The term is derived from "nean," and this from "neos" which denotes "one recently born, young, youthful," and indicates the young or recent in point of time. Hence the word also occurs as descriptive of "youths, young attendants, and servants." It is equivalent to our colloquial "boy, lad, lass" (cf. Gen. 37:2; Exod. 33:11; 1 Sam. 17:33), and may thus also designate a young maid of less than twenty years of age. It is not possible therefore to use the Septuagint version's word "neanis" for *almah*, to show that *almah* describes a "young woman" and not a "virgin."

Proceeding upon the basis of the equitable assumption that Miriam was approximately fifteen years of age at the time when the event recorded in Exodus 2:1-8 took place, it is therefore reasonable to believe that she was a "virgin," having not at this age known a man. Nothing in the Exodus 2:8 passage even remotely suggests that the word *almah*, referring to the sister of Moses, means anything other than "virgin." If Miriam was of such age as would warrant a description of her as an unmarried young woman, or if she was married at the time of this event, the word *almah* would not have been used by Moses writing under inspiration. It is logical to assume that, under such circumstances, the word *nah-arah* (as in Ruth 4:12) would have been used, or the common term *ish-shah* referring to a wife (as in Ruth 3:11). The word *almah* describes Miriam in the definitive way which best and most accurately and appropriately fits the young "maid" whom God with His all-wise provi-

16

dence used. Miriam was divinely selected in the pure state of her girlhood to exercise an uncorrupted family bond and a loving dexterity in behalf of her infant brother who was destined in the plan of God to become the leader of Israel.

3, 4. THE USE OF *almah* IN 1 CHRONICLES 15:20 AND PSALM 46:1.

The plural form *alamoth* occurs in both these texts, and is used in the same way in each passage, so the two references may be considered together. In 1 Chronicles 15:20 the word appears in the last line of the text itself, "with psalteries on *Alamoth*." As for the use of the term in Psalm 46:1, it should be pointed out that the KJV shows the word in the inscription of the Psalm, "A Song upon Alamoth," while the Hebrew text includes the words of the inscription in verse 1.

In these passages the term shows the value attached to music by the Hebrew people and the important place afforded it in the divine services of worship. The word has been taken by some to signify the virgin tone or pitch of the voices of young maidens, that is, as higher than those of men; hence "soprano" in contrast to the lower octave of "tenor" or "bass." This is a plausible view held by numerous writers, but far from convincing. There is no good reason to assume that the word could not refer to the "singers" or "players" themselves. For even if its occurrence in these texts is taken as a technical expression of the Hebrew music to de-

17

note the soprano voices, it thus links the soprano voices to soprano singers and points to the singers as "virgins." While perhaps an unequivocal identification of the term *alamoth* as "virgins" may not here be possible, neither does its use offer the slightest implication that such is not the meaning. In fact, the use of *alamoth* in these passages rather strongly suggests that the word is to be rendered "virgins." Moreover, it must be kept in mind that the use of a word, not its etymology, finally determines its meaning. Although *almah* is not the common word for "virgin," it cannot be shown that its use ever denotes anything other than "virgin."

5. THE USE OF *almah* IN PSALM 68:25.

The significance of *almah* in this text, where it appears for "damsels" (KJV), is best understood against the background and in the setting of the whole Psalm. Locally, Psalm 68, like Psalm 18 which it resembles, was occasioned and written in celebration of a noteworthy and signal military victory. Perhaps the triumph was the one recorded in 2 Samuel 12:26-31, which describes the highly successful campaign against the Ammonites and which was the last great important war of David's reign. The Psalm opens with a song of praise to God as the deliverer of the righteous and author of victory. It follows with references to His power, providence, and provision for His people in varied periods of their experience, confirmation of the kingdom by the victory just achieved, and a description of the triumphant procession in joyful commemoration of the event.

A natural and fitting part of that triumphant procession as it moved toward the temple, was the large chorus of singers and the group of musicians who played upon instruments. The true sense of the Hebrew in verse 25 is that the singers and the instrumentalists were surrounded by young maids tapping rhythmically upon timbrels. It was not customary for *young married women* to perform this service, so the term *alamoth* is appropriate as designating the *young virgin maids* whose joyous participation in such a festive celebration is thus specifically described. Had the Psalmist intended to denote the service as performed merely by *young women,* or by *young married women,* he would surely have used the common term *nah-arah,* which clearly expresses that idea.

The Psalm is also prophetic in character and is thus a foretaste of universal conquest yet to come. Its prophetical nature has to do with the rejoicing of the saved remnant of Israel and the establishment of the Messianic Kingdom of the Lord Jesus Christ at the end of this age. The rejoicing of redeemed Israel is prominent, and the Messianic character of the Psalm is emphasized by the unmistakable reference to Christ in verses 16-20; His dwelling-place, verse 16; His deputies, verse 17; His descent, verse 18; His death, resurrection and ascension, verse 18; His deliverance from death, verses 19, 20. The triumphal pageant in verses 22-29 is fit-

ting as celebrating the establishment of the Kingdom (Rev. 11:15; 19:6), and the entire section in
verses 19-35 is descriptive of the glorious reign of
the Lord Jesus Christ in the millennial era.

It is not possible, nor is it necessary, to make a
positive identification of these virgin maidens (*alamoth*) in the prophetic view of this Psalm. However their action is certainly indicative of their joy
and is expressive of their blessedness because of the
presence of the Messiah and the place of redeemed
Israel in the Kingdom. In this setting and amid
such circumstances the term *alamoth* is most fitting
and appropriate, and it is utterly impossible for
anyone to prove that, in such an occurrence of the
word, *almah* means anything else than "virgin."

6. THE USE OF *almah* IN PROVERBS 30:19.

There is nothing in this passage to contradict
the meaning of *almah* as "virgin." Rather all the
indications point to the translation "virgin" as
being correct. Verses 18-20 form a paragraph beginning with the writer's reference to three things
which are too "wonderful" (Hebrew, *pah-lah*,
"great" in the sense of being difficult to comprehend). Then the writer adds a fourth, to which the
three previous things lead, and of which he says:
"I know not" (Hebrew, *yadah*, "I cannot understand"). The text is very much like Job 42:3, in
which Job states: "Therefore have I uttered that
which I understand not; things too wonderful for
me, which I knew not." The Hebrew words "won-

derful" and "knew" are the same as the comparable terms in Proverbs 30:18.

The first three things belong to the realm of nature, but are designed as comparisons for the illustration of the fourth, giving significance and weight to it. These are actions such as leave no visible trace behind them, and the whole statement thus gathers up its force into an unusual climax: "The way of a man with a maid." The noun "man" is the Hebrew *geber*, which is not the usual way of expressing "man," but is a word used much less frequently than *ahdam* or *iysh*, which are the common Hebrew terms for "man." The word *geber* refers to a "mighty man, a warrior," describing *a man in his strength*, who prevails, overpowers, subdues. It is precisely the word which suits the point in the text. Moreover, the preposition prefixed to the feminine *almah* is "beh" which generally expresses the idea "in," although it is sometimes rendered "with, among, as, against." However, the common use is that of "in"—the equivalent of the Greek *en*. Hence the thought of the man's unlawful intercourse with the maiden is intensified and the intimate nature of the relationship rendered more forceful. The poignant truth which strikes the writer's mind is the sinful act of unchaste intercourse to which the first three comparisons are linked, and of which the words "the way of a man with a maid" speak. The proverb describes the seduction of a virgin maiden, who yields to the persuasive charm and forceful passion of her seducer and the insidious arts by which he saps her principles and inflames her passions in an hour of uncontrolled desire. Such an act requires secrecy and leaves no outward sign by which it is generally recognized, so it escapes man's knowledge. Those who come in contact with the guilty parties may see no more trace of the sin than they would see of an eagle's course, a serpent's track, or a ship's passage.

This is prefaced by the first three proverbial statements which lead on to the fourth. The wild, savage freedom of the eagle's flight, the subtle secret of the serpent's trail, and the tempestuous voyage of a ship in a great sea are suggestive of uncontrolled passion and selfish vice. It is further exemplified and confirmed in the following verse of the paragraph (v. 20). What the writer has said concerning the man and his way with the maid in verse 19, he now applies to the practiced adulteress whose sin cannot be traced. As she sins in secret intercourse with men, and as there is no outward proof of her guilt, she boldly denies it.

Hence the rendering of the word *almah* in this text is without doubt rightfully "virgin." The term does not mean "widow," or "married woman," or "woman in general" or even "young unmarried woman." It is utterly impossible to disprove the translation of the word as "virgin."

7, 8. THE USE OF *almah* IN THE SONG OF SOLOMON 1:3 AND 6:8.

The word *almah* should not be altered in these

passages to mean "young woman" whether married or not, in order to express the love of all young women for King Solomon—as Redford in the *Pulpit Commentary* (Song of Solomon, p. 3) states: "Thou art the delight of all the young." The Song of Solomon is an exquisite book of Holy Scripture, setting forth the expression and description of true, pure marital love in all of its beauty and delicacy. The content of the book is somewhat mysterious and difficult of exact interpretation, but no reason may thus be afforded for changing the translation of *almah* from its meaning in the other texts where it occurs as "virgin."

It is a fact that the gynaeceum, or harem, of the oriental kings was always an essential and special part of the monarchial palace (cf. 1 Kings 7:8-10). In many of the palaces, particularly those of the Persian kings, it was very extensive, since the Persian rulers often maintained besides their legitimate wives, as many as 300 or 400 concubines. There were also in these oriental courts groups of young virgin maidens, who were selected from the various parts of the empire and brought into the royal court. These virgins were beautiful young maidens, whose purpose was to please the king, and to be attendants and maids of the harem. Some of these maidens might be exalted by the king to be concubines, if he chose to do so, or he might select from them another legitimate wife or queen. A good illustration of this point is found in Esther 2:1-20, where the word for "virgin" is *bethulah*. From this passage it appears clear that the "virgins" (Hebrew, *bethuloth*) were placed in their own chambers in the harem under the supervision of Hegai (v. 3), and the concubines occupied another part of the harem under the special oversight of Shaashgaz (v. 12-14).

It is evident from the Song of Solomon 1:3 and 6:8, that there were also young virgin maidens (Hebrew, *alamoth*) in the court of King Solomon. Perhaps the nature of this extraordinarily beautiful and exquisite book of Holy Scripture is in part explanatory of the Holy Spirit's use of *almah* rather than *bethulah*. In neither passage does the definite article appear with the noun *alamoth*, hence not setting forth a special class by itself. The plural noun without the article rather designates simply "virgins," indicating kind and character, such as the Shulamite herself. She has apparently but recently been brought into the circle of virgin maidens of the royal court, and accounts to herself for the fact that many other virgin maidens are attendant upon the king with admiring devotion and love. These "virgins" may be a part of the harem, or they may be simply maids of the court, attendants in the harem. But whatever their purpose and position with reference to the court, they are *alamoth*, "virgins," and not merely "young women" whether virgins or not, and there is nothing to show otherwise.

II

An Examination of the Use of Almah in Isaiah 7:14

The great historic fact that our Lord Jesus Christ was conceived by the Holy Spirit and born of the virgin Mary is one of the great fundamental doctrinal truths of the Christian faith, and must be received, believed and confessed by every true child of God. While there is considerable material which forms the Biblical basis for the truth of the virgin birth of Christ, it is nevertheless true that the great prophecy in Isaiah 7:14 is a key passage in the consideration of the doctrine. In the KJV the important second clause reads: "Behold, a virgin shall conceive and bear a son." The word properly rendered "virgin" is the Hebrew *almah*—the same word which occurs in the eight passages previously considered. The RSV takes the English word out of the clause and translates *almah* as "a young woman," while the NEB renders the whole clause: "Behold, *a young woman* is with child." In the RSV the word "virgin" is relegated to a footnote as a secondary rendering, by which the revisers reveal their preference for the translation "young woman," and thus clearly display their attitude toward this prophecy and the great truth of the Virgin Birth itself. If they truly believed the doctrine of Christ's virgin birth, they would not hesitate to confess it (1 John 4:2, 3). Dr. McClain remarks

> . . . if the word *virgin* was a possible translation of the Hebrew word, then there could be no valid reason for not leaving the word *virgin* in the verse, unless they were determined to exclude from the prophecy any reference to the birth of Christ.[1]

The same commentary may be applied to the editors of the NEB, and their removal of the word "virgin" from the text of Isaiah 7:14. So, while *almah* is used in the eight other passages it is here in Isaiah 7:14 that the battle rages, and the liberal critics continue to center their attack. Therefore let us consider carefully the use of *almah* in this significant prophecy.

1. THE WORD *almah* ITSELF, IN ITS NATURE AND USAGE, ATTESTS ITS TRUE MEANING.

It has been shown in the preceding brief consideration of *almah* in the eight other passages where it occurs, that it is impossible for anyone to

---

1 Dr. Alva J. McClain, op. cit., p. 138.

prove in any of these occurrences that the word *almah* means anything else than "virgin." All the evidence points to "virgin" as the meaning of the word. The noun itself is the feminine form of the Hebrew *ehlem*, which describes something that is kept out of sight, and which in turn is derived from the verb *ahlam*, which means "to veil from sight," to conceal or keep hidden. In Leviticus 4:13 the verb describes a sin that is "hidden" from the eyes of the assembly of Israel. Deuteronomy 22:1 speaks of one who "hides" himself, that is, withholds help from his brother. First Kings 10:3 states that King Solomon answered all the questions of the Queen of Sheba, and "there was not anything *hidden* from the king, which he told her not." In Job 42:3, the verb appears in the first clause where Job asks of God concerning anyone who *"hideth counsel"* without knowledge. And the Psalmist, in Psalm 10:1, cries out to God: "Why *hidest* thou thyself in times of trouble?" The feminine noun *almah* taken from this verb form clearly describes a young maiden who has been kept secluded and hidden in the sense that she has been guarded from the vices and evils of the world, and withheld from intimacy and intercourse with men.

Dr. Robert Dick Wilson, perhaps the greatest linguistic scholar of our modern age, stated unequivocally after prolonged and careful study of all the available evidence, that the KJV translation of "virgin" for the word *almah* in Isaiah 7:14 and the other texts where it occurs, is correct and proper.

This rendering was also given unqualified support by Dr. James Orr, a scholar of great learning and knowledge of the Biblical languages. Dr. J. Gresham Machen, another renowned scholar and learned defender of the faith, testified to the meaning of *almah* as "virgin." And the statement of Martin Luther still stands unchallenged and unforgettable: "If any Jew or Christian can prove to me that in any passage of Scripture where it occurs, *almah* means 'married woman,' I will give him a hundred florins, although God alone knows where I shall get them." Finally, the striking comment of R. A. Bertram in the *Homiletical Commentary on the Prophecies of Isaiah,* at Isaiah 7:14, is most impressive:

> But the word here translated "virgin" signifies, in every other part of the Old Testament, *a woman who hath not known a man.* And the consequence from hence is, that the words "a virgin shall conceive, and bear a son" cannot be applied properly to Isaiah's wife. As it is here affirmed that the original word *almah* signifies "virgin" in every other text, it should be just observed that the text in the book of Proverbs (30:18, 19) which has been often brought to prove the contrary, is not here forgotten; and that even *that* text might (if the nature of this discourse would permit) be explained fairly and to satisfaction, in a manner perfectly consistent with the preceding assertion.[1]

---

1 R. A. Bertram, *Homiletical Commentary on the Prophecies of Isaiah*, 7:13-16, (New York: Funk & Wagnalls Publishing Co., 1892), p. 161.

2. It is significant that the word *almah* is used instead of *bethulah* which is the Hebrew term generally used to designate "virgin."

Much is made of this fact by the modern critical scholars, and it is urged that if "virgin" had been intended in Isaiah 7:14, the word *bethulah* would have been used. But as previously indicated, there is no place among the nine occurrences of *almah* where the word can be said to clearly designate a woman who was not a virgin. It is true that *bethulah* is the Hebrew word most frequently used to denote a virgin. There are some fifty-nine clear uses of the word, twelve times rendered "maid, maiden, maidens," and forty-seven times translated "virgin, virgins, virginity," in contrast to the nine occurrences of *almah*. However, it is noteworthy that neither word is ever rendered "wife, woman, widow," and never clearly designates "married woman," except perhaps in Joel 1:8, "Lament like a *virgin* girded with sackcloth for the husband of her youth." But even here, the sense is not absolute, for the case may not refer specifically to a married woman who has lost her husband still in youth, but may indicate the case of a virgin maid betrothed to a young man who dies before the marriage is consummated.

If Isaiah had used the word *bethulah* instead of *almah*, it would admittedly have been to use the more usual term, but it would not have been more explicit than *almah*. If it had been the intention of the prophet, writing under inspiration, to designate

29

merely a "young woman" and not a "virgin," the Hebrew word *nah⸗arah*, to which previous reference has been made, would have most suitably and clearly expressed the point. Machen states that while *bethulah* is the usual and unmistakable Hebrew term for "virgin," and even if it could be claimed that almah does not etymologically indicate virginity as precisely as *bethulah* does,

> ...on the other hand one may well doubt, in view of the usage, that it was a natural word to use of anyone who was not in point of fact a virgin....If a married woman were referred to in Isaiah 7:14, it does seem as though some other word than *almah* would naturally be used.[1]

The difference between the two words, *almah* and *bethulah,* seems to be that *bethulah* suggests the state of a maiden who is living with her parents, and whose marriage is not yet impending. *Almah* indicates a maid who has been withheld from intimacy with a man, but who is approaching readiness to engage in marriage. Despite the cavils and criticisms against the rendering of *almah* as "virgin," the use of the word here in Isaiah 7:14, together with other evidence for its meaning, makes it clear that the event foretold in this prophecy was not a birth in the ordinary course of nature. But *almah* designates "virgin" as definitely and distinctly as she could be by a single Hebrew word.

---

1 Dr. J. Gresham Machen, *The Virgin Birth of Christ,* (New York: Harper and Brothers, Publishers, 1930) , pp. 288-289.

Had *bethulah* been used, the translation "virgin" would have been clear, but in view of the usage of *almah* and other points of evidence, the term *almah* makes the matter even clearer and more distinctive.

3. It should be carefully noted that the noun *almah* carries the definite article.

The Hebrew expression is literally *ha-almah*, an important point, for the translation is therefore *"the* virgin," and not *"a* virgin." This is likewise true in the Septuagint version, and in Matthew's quotation of the prophecy. The function of the definite article in the Hebrew is much the same as in the Greek—to particularize, and to point out individual identity. The noun with the article is definite and distinguished. Critical scholars see little that is favorable here in the articular noun and still insist that the translation should be "young woman." But the testimony of the definite article cannot be so easily brushed aside and ignored. The fact remains that *ha-almah* is *"the* virgin," thus pointing to a particular virgin maiden. A definite virgin is in view and this is an indication of her identity.

The Gospel of Matthew pinpoints this identity and declares in unmistakable terms that Isaiah 7:14 is the prophecy of the Virgin Birth of the Lord Jesus Christ. "All this was done that it might be fulfilled which was spoken by the Lord through the prophet saying, 'Behold, *the* virgin shall be with child, and shall bring forth a son, and they shall

31

call his name Immanuel" (Matt. 1:22, 23, LT[1]).

Ha-almah (the virgin) of Isaiah 7:14 finds its counterpart in *hei parthenos* (*the* virgin) of Matthew 1:23. There can be no mistake in the identification of these terms or in the fulfillment of the one in the other. *The* virgin (*ha-almah*) of Isaiah 7:14, concerning whom it was prophesied that she would conceive and bear a son whose name would be called "Emmanuel," is *the* virgin (*hei parthenos*) of Matthew 1:23, concerning whom it is stated clearly that she—Mary, espoused to Joseph—is the divinely-chosen maiden in whom the great prophecy of Isaiah 7:14 was fulfilled.

4. IT IS MOST IMPORTANT TO NOTE THE VERBAL EXPRESSION IN THE PROPHECY, WHICH DENOTES THE PREGNANCY OF *ha-almah.*

The standard translation of the prophetic statement as set forth in the KJV is: "A virgin shall conceive and bear a son...." The future time element in the verbal "shall conceive" has been commonly accepted as essential to the messianic view of the prophecy, hence many commentators have simply followed, one after the other, in the KJV rendering. However, the expression "shall conceive" is neither a verb nor a participle, but a *feminine adjective, harah,* used with an active participle ren-

---

1 LT indicates a literal translation of the original language by the author and will be referred to throughout the rest of the book in this way.

dered "bearing," which denotes that the verbal time element is *present* rather than *future*. Over a hundred years ago, J. A. Alexander pointed out this important fact in his splendid commentary on Isaiah:

> As to the form of the expression it will only be necessary further to remark that *harah* is not a verb or participle, but a feminine adjective, signifying "pregnant," and here connected with an active participle, to denote that the object is described as present to the prophet's view. "Behold the virgin, pregnant, and bringing forth a son, and she calls his name Immanuel." The future form adopted by the Septuagint is retained in the New Testament because the words are there considered simply as a prophecy; but in order to exhibit the full force which they have in their original connection, the present form must be restored.[1]

This present time element is very important to the interpretation of the prophecy, and leads to the inescapable conclusion that Isaiah 7:14 is unquestionably a picture of the virgin birth of Christ. For God gives the prophet to see this *almah* as *already* pregnant and about to bear a son. In the prophetic view it is not a pregnancy that will take place at a future time, but *the almah is now pregnant*. This means that since the *almah* is already pregnant and about to bear a son, *she is still a virgin*, even though

---

1 Joseph Addison Alexander, *Commentary on the Prophecies of Isaiah*, (Grand Rapids, Michigan: Zondervan Publishing House, 1953 Edition), p. 172.

she is about to become a mother. How is such a thing possible? How is it that the *almah* can remain a virgin, and yet be pregnant at the same time? The answer is clear: the son is miraculously conceived and born without the participation of a human father, and in spite of the pregnancy, the mother is still a virgin. If the time element in the verb action were actually future, there could be no certainty that the virgin who would sometime in the future become pregnant and bear a son, would still be a virgin. But the present tense of the verbal expression reveals that the *almah* is now already with child, and she is still both virgin and mother. This is one of the most remarkable grammatical structures in all the Holy Scriptures. The only conclusion which can possibly be drawn is that what God has set forth here is the announcement of the virgin birth of our Lord Jesus Christ. If this is not a reference to the one and only miraculous event of its kind in all history—the only virgin birth that has ever occurred, or ever will occur—then it is an inexplicable fantasy of contradiction and deceit. But the remarkable form of the Hebrew text in this great statement leaves no doubt as to its meaning: "Behold, the virgin, pregnant and bearing a son. . . ." Matthew clearly identifies the *almah* as Mary, the mother of Jesus, who alone meets all the qualifications for the fulfillment of this prophecy.

5. THE GOSPEL OF MATTHEW SUPPLIES AMPLE PROOF THAT ISAIAH 7:14 IS THE PROPHECY OF THE VIRGIN BIRTH OF CHRIST.

It has already been pointed out that Matthew, when quoting the prophecy in Isaiah 7:14, uses the Greek word *parthenos* (Matt. 1:23), with the definite article, to translate the Hebrew articular noun *ha-almah*. And as Dr. McClain remarks: "Matthew wrote by immediate inspiration of the Holy Spirit." The meaning of *hei parthenos* is indisputable. It is "*the* virgin"—the very one of Isaiah 7:14. Matthew's words constitute incontrovertible proof:

> Now all this was done, that it might be fulfilled which was spoken by the Lord through the prophet, saying, "Behold, the virgin shall be with child..." (Matt. 1:22, 23—LT).

The account of Matthew settles any lingering doubt with respect to the prophecy in Isaiah 7:14, and concerning the proper meaning and translation of the Hebrew noun *almah*.

In addition to the all-important *hei parthenos*, there are other significant facts in Matthew's record which support the testimony of *hei parthenos*, and help to develop the meaning and significance of *ha-almah*. Each of these repudiate the critical denials of the virgin birth of Christ, and establish the doctrine beyond all question. Four particular details require special attention.

(1) *The change of expression in Matthew 1:16 is most significant.*

Throughout the entire preface, verses 1-15, the verb "begot" is used again and again. But at verse 16 it makes a halt and the expression changes with a remarkable grammatical construction. In marked contrast with the regular begetting of one ancestor by another, we are told by Matthew that the last thus begotten was Joseph, "the husband of Mary *of whom* was born Jesus, who is called Christ." It is the prepositional phrase "of whom" that is of particular significance here, for the preposition is *ek,* denoting source, while the pronoun is singular and in the feminine gender (*heis*), pointing clearly and remarkably to Mary *only*. Our Lord Jesus Christ was born (*egenneithei*) of his mother *alone*, and not by the usual method of natural generation as the result of the sexual union of Joseph and Mary. How this took place follows immediately. The name "Jesus" was very frequently used among Jewish families. Hence the participial clause is added: "The one called Christ." This clause tells us that the name "Christ" was the second rightful and official name belonging to the Lord. Thus Matthew's genealogy shows Joseph as the *legal* father of the Lord Jesus Christ, which makes Christ legally the heir of David and Abraham. Lenski states:

> If Jesus had been born without a legal father, of Mary without a legal husband, his legal right to the inheritance from Abraham and David by virtue of the divine promise would have been void. In addition to the legal standing of Jesus as the rightful, legal son of Joseph, we may note the protection this standing secured for his mother and for himself. The two records of Matthew and Luke vividly bring out this point.[1]

---

1 R.C.H. Lenski, *The Interpretation of Matthew* (Columbus, Ohio: The Wartburg Press, 1943), p. 34.

But the RSV has placed a footnote related to verse 16 in the margin, which reads: "Other ancient authorities read: Joseph, to whom was betrothed the virgin Mary, was the father of Jesus who is called Christ."[1] This is a clear and unmistakable statement that Joseph was the father of Jesus Christ. However, it is a plain misrepresentation of the truth, for the modernist revisers say this rendering occurs in "other authorities" when the fact is that it is found in only one old version—the Sinaitic Syriac Version, discovered in 1892. Lenski comments:

> Here we meet a typical example of critical methods. Of all the ancient texts in existence, including all the ancient versions, one (usually identified by the symbol *Ss*), is singled out as containing a reading which the critics use to rid themselves of the virgin birth. All Greek texts and all other versions are set aside, for this one Syriac translation, the codex *Ss* and its reading, is made *the original reading*, and all other texts are regarded as an accommodation to the doctrine of the Virgin Birth.[2]

The NEB is more truthful in its footnote on verse 16 than the RSV, since it states: *"One early witness has:* Joseph, to whom Mary, a virgin, was

---

1 This footnote appears in the RSV Bible revised in 1952, copyrighted by the Division of Christian Education of the National Council of Churches of Christ in the United States of America.
It also appears in the NEB New Testament, where it reads, "...one early witness has 'Joseph, and Joseph, to whom Mary, a virgin, was betrothed, was the father of....'"

2. R.C.H. Lenski, op. cit., p. 34.

betrothed, was the father of Jesus...." The question must certainly be asked: Why did the revisers carefully choose this one variant reading from the many ancient versions, and put it in the RSV margin, when it has practically no worthwhile evidence at all? Machen's comments on the Syriac Version are of special interest at this point:

> It is not true therefore, as has sometimes been popularly supposed, that the Sinaitic Syriac is our earliest copy of the Gospels; for two of the Greek Manuscripts, the Codex Vaticanus and the Codex Sinaiticus, are to be dated earlier still....The view therefore that the Sinaitic Syriac at Matthew 1:16 represents the original text of the Gospel can be maintained only by textual criticism of the most adventurous and unscientific mind. The reading of the Sinaitic Syriac cannot with any certainty be traced back of A.D. 400, while the common reading is clearly attested at the beginning of the third century, and certainly was present considerably before that time....At any rate ...the reading of the Sinaitic Syriac at Matthew 1:16 is accordingly without bearing upon the question of the historicity of the virgin birth....[1]

Furthermore, this footnote did not appear in the 1946 edition of the RSV New Testament, but was placed into the New Testament text when the entire RSV Bible was published in 1952. This cannot possibly be a coincidence or innocent mistake, but it speaks plainly of purpose and intent on the part of the revising committee, and reveals the theological bias of these liberals against the virgin

1 J. Gresham Machen, op. cit., pp. 177-186.

birth of Christ. The revisers have deliberately ignored the true reading of the Greek text in verse 16 —*Marias ex heis egenneithei Ieisous*: "Mary, out of whom [only and alone] Jesus was born."

(2) *The manner of Christ's conception is described in Matthew* 1:18.

The first clause reads: "Now the birth of Jesus Christ was on this wise" (KJV), or "in this way" (New Scofield edition). The name "the Christ" heads the statement. The genitive articular proper noun *tou christou* is placed first in the sentence, thus bearing the significant emphasis. It is the generation of *the one called Christ* that is here recorded. Hence, this emphasis upon the One whose name is Christ, prepares the way for the description of His unique entrance into the world. For this is the sense of the words that follow. He who would be *the Christ,* the great personal culmination and fulfillment of the divine promises, would in His very birth exceed all His human ancestors. In fact, His birth would far surpass all births to come as well. The word "birth" is the Greek *genesis* in the sense of origin, and the predicate "was on this wise" is *houtos ein,* which means "was in this manner." It is *the manner* of the origin which Matthew emphasizes. No other person ever had an origin *in this manner*. No one else was ever born of a virgin mother without the participation of a human father.

But Matthew says further: "When as his mother Mary was espoused to Joseph, *before they came together,* she was found with child of the Holy Ghost." In Jewish custom, a period of time was required between the betrothal and the coming together of husband and wife. By inspiration, Matthew places his readers directly into the interval between the betrothal of Joseph and Mary and their conjugal union, when he records the significant words *prin ei sunelthein autous,* "before they came together." Before the bringing of Mary as the bride of Joseph to the home of her husband ever took place and before the two had come together as husband and wife, "she was found with child of the Holy Spirit."

We do not know how long after the betrothal, or how soon before the planned and expected coming together of husband and wife, Joseph discovered Mary's pregnancy. However, the point is immaterial for Matthew's narrative and for our purpose here. It is to be expected that Joseph would look happily forward to the festive day when he would go and take his wife and bring her into his own home. Thus when he discovered that she was pregnant before they had come together, surely it struck him at first as a dreadful calamity: his espoused wife was with child. But at the proper moment God intervened, and sent His angel to Joseph, to remove the fears and misgivings, for they had no foundation in reality. "Joseph, son of David, fear not to take possession of Mary, thy wife; for what was conceived in her is of the Holy Spirit" (Matt. 1:20— LT).

This description of Mary's condition sheds the full light of divine truth upon the fact here recorded. Here is the full significance of *ha-almah* in Isaiah 7:14. Before Joseph and Mary had ever been united as husband and wife in sexual union, while Mary was still in her virginal state, that state described by *almah*, she was found with child *ek pneumatos hagious*, "out of the Holy Spirit." This is the great reality of which the angel had previously spoken to Mary at the occasion of the annunciation of the divine choice of Mary as the mother of the child Jesus (Luke 1:24-35). It is also the answer to Mary's question: "How shall this be, *seeing I know not a man?*" The reply was: "The Holy Ghost shall come upon thee, and the power of the Highest shall overshadow thee..." (Luke 1:34, 35).

(3) *Matthew's account repeats the divine source of the conception in the virgin's womb.*

Having stated clearly that the virgin Mary "was found with child *of the Holy Ghost*" (1:18), just a few sentences later Matthew reiterates: "for that which is conceived in her is *of the Holy Ghost*" (1:20). The Apostolic Creed states: "conceived *of the Holy Ghost*," and the Nicene Creed reads: "Incarnate *by the Holy Ghost* of the virgin Mary." There is no definite article with "Holy Ghost" in the original text, but none is needed in this case. The phrase, both in verse 18 and in verse 20, is in the form of a title, so may or may not carry the article "the." Moreover, the construction without the definite article characterizes the source of the conception. It denotes kind and quality, and tells us that the miraculous conception in the womb of the virgin Mary was *a Holy Spirit kind of work*. It did not bear the character of human generation, but rather the character of the presence and power of God the Holy Spirit. The entire conception was wrought by the omnipotent power and operation of the Holy Spirit of God. Liberal unitarian views deny the plain grammatical fact in order to change the third person of the Godhead into the impersonal power of an impersonal God. But the fact first set forth in *ha-almah* of Isaiah 7:14, then recorded as to fulfillment in Matthew 1:18-25, and described as to character as the work of the Holy Spirit of God, still stands, and no critical attack can abolish it.

The great mystery of the miraculous conception and virgin birth of the Lord Jesus Christ is expressed by the angel (Matt. 1:20) in the simplest words. This is one of the clearest and most definite marks of inspiration. The profound facts and verities which the human mind cannot ever fully comprehend, are expressed in terms of utter simplicity, yet with perfect adequacy. In every case, *the fact* is set forth beyond all doubt *as fact*, yet *how* this or that can possibly be is left unrevealed. Who can understand *how* the conception in the womb of the virgin took place *ek pneumatos hagiou*, "out of the Holy Spirit"? We do not fully understand just how an ordinary human being with his own personality and with all his normal physical and mental peculiarities is conceived in the common act of procreation. An ordinary human conception is also, in spite of all our science, as great a mystery as ever— a new person, an immortal soul, suddenly coming into existence. This is an everyday miracle, but the miracle of the virgin birth is veiled in mystery. This conception was wrought *ek pneumatos hagiou,* "out of the Holy Spirit." This we know; beyond this we cannot go, but the fact stands forth. Lenski states:

> What *ek* contains is voiced confessionally: The most blessed virgin bore not a mere man, but as the angel testifies, such a man as is truly the Son of the Most High God, who showed His divine majesty even in His mother's womb, inasmuch as He was born of a virgin, with her virginity inviolate.[1]

(4) *Matthew attests the fulfillment of Isaiah 7:14, and confirms the name given to Christ in the prophecy.*

The great prophetic announcement concerning the virgin, *ha-almah,* that she would conceive and bear a son who would be called "Immanuel" (*God with us*) in Isaiah 7:14, has its fulfillment in the virgin conception and birth of the Son of God who thus became *Immanuel.* Matthew adds the Greek *meth' heimon ho theos* (*God with us*), so that all his readers would realize the full significance of the

---

1 R.C.H. Lenski, op. cit., p. 48.

name. The comment of Delitzsch is very fitting:

> He is God in bodily presentation, therefore a
> miracle in the form of a superhuman person.
> We would not dare to say this, because it tran-
> scends the Old Testament plane of knowledge,
> but the prophet himself says so, Isaiah 9:6; 10:21;
> his statement is as clear as possible, we dare not
> darken it in the interest of a preconceived con-
> struction of history. The incarnation is indeed
> a veiled mystery in the Old Testament but the
> veil is not so dense that it admits of no rays strik-
> ing through. A ray of this kind, cast by the Spirit
> of prophecy into the spirit of the prophet, is this
> prophecy concerning Immanuel. But if the Mes-
> siah is Immanuel in the sense that, as the prophet
> explicitly says, he is himself *El* (God), then his
> birth must also be a miraculous one....[1]

Such is the birth prophesied in Isaiah 7:14, and
recorded in Matthew 1:18-25, of the One whose
name was *Immanuel*. It is true that the name
Immanuel is used of God to signify His providential presence with His people to deliver them
from some great danger or perilous situation, as in
Isaiah 43:2 and Jeremiah 1:8. But the word cannot
be restricted to that which is only providential, and
certainly in the great prophecy of Isaiah 7:14, expresses the *personal* presence of the Messiah Himself. J. A. Alexander says:

> So too the name *Immanuel*, although it might be
> used to signify God's *providential* presence mere-

---

1 Quotation from Dr. Franz Delitzsch, in *The Interpretation
of Matthew*, by R.C.H. Lenski, pp. 54-55.

ly, has a latitude and pregnancy of meaning which can scarcely be fortuitous, and which combined with all the rest, makes the conclusion almost unavoidable that it was here intended to express a *personal* as well as a *providential* presence.[1]

The question as to why Christ was never actually called "Immanuel" is answered by the editors of the new edition of the Scofield Bible in footnote 4, on page 992:

> Why was Jesus not actually called "Immanuel"? According to Hebrew usage the name does not represent a title but a characterization, as in Isaiah 1:26 and 9:6. The name "Immanuel" shows that He really was "God with us." Thus the deity of Christ is stressed at the very beginning of Matthew.

6. The Septuagint Version supports the translation of *almah* as "virgin."

This Version is a translation of the Old Testament Scriptures into the Greek language for the benefit of dispersed Greek-speaking Jews of Alexandria and Egypt, and surrounding areas. The work of translation was done by a group of prominent Jewish scholars in Alexandria, begun in approximately 280 b.c., and finally completed about 200 b.c. Its importance should be carefully noted because: (1) It is the oldest translation of the Old Testament Scriptures into another language. (2) Its

---

1 J. A. Alexander, op. cit., p. 168.

45

object was to make the Old Testament Scriptures plain to the common people. (3) It released the great eternal verities of God, the Messiah, redemption, etc., from the sole charge of the Hebrew people and language, and gave them to the world through the Greek language.

It is a most remarkable fact that when the translators of this ancient version dealt with Isaiah 7:14, they rendered the Hebrew word *almah* into the Greek text by the Greek word *parthenos,* the meaning of which cannot be denied. It means "virgin," and this meaning cannot be manipulated or changed. Now it is surely sensible to assume that Jewish scholars should know best how to translate their own language, particularly their own Scriptures, hence their translation of *almah* by the Greek *parthenos* is most significant. As Dr. McClain has said:

> To any person with a fair share of common sense, it would seem that those Jewish scholars living 200 years before Christ should have known better how to translate their own language, and specifically the Book of Isaiah, than men far removed in time by 2,000 years from them.[1]

7. THE RECORD IN THE GOSPEL OF LUKE IS EXPLANATORY OF THE SIGNIFICANCE OF THE WORD *almah.*

The angelic annunciation of God's choice of the virgin Mary is recorded in Luke 1:26-38, where the interpretation of the Hebrew word *almah* in Isaiah

---

1 Alva J. McClain, op. cit., pp. 138-139.

46

7:14 is remarkably set forth:

(1) *By the use of the word parthenos for "virgin" in verse* 27.

Matthew uses this word with the definite article, but it occurs in Luke without the article, which emphasizes the *kind* and *character* of the maiden. It is significant that Luke uses the word *parthenos* twice in verse 27, to emphasize particularly the fact of Mary's virginity. It seems that Luke is purposely insisting on this point by the repetition of the word. She was unquestionably a virgin, now in readiness for her marriage to Joseph. The truth of the Virgin Birth must have been profoundly impressed in the mind of Luke, for otherwise the narration is most unnatural. Mary is described as having been betrothed to a man named "Joseph" but we must understand this from the Jewish standpoint. The Jewish betrothal was a public event, and embodied all the essentials of the marriage vows. No further promises followed, and no additional vows were made. By virtue of the betrothal, the bridegroom and the bride virtually became husband and wife, as Matthew 1:20 indicates. It was necessary only that at the set time the bridegroom should come, take his bride, celebrate, and live with her. It is incorrect to regard the "husband" and the "wife" as proleptic terms designating the husband and wife to be. This is interpreting the Jewish procedure in terms of our modern conception of engagement. With us a betrothal is merely an engagement, and not marriage. It is a pledge of future marriage, and the binding marriage vows are not spoken until the marriage ceremony itself takes place. Then the consummation of the marriage follows. But the Jewish betrothal was the marriage itself, and Jewish custom required an interval between the betrothal and the bringing home of the bride to her husband's house. No further religious ceremony and no additional vows of any kind accompanied this home bringing, although it was made a festive occasion with a procession and a feast to follow. After this the consummation of the marriage would come. Luke stresses the kind of maiden Mary was—*a virgin*, ready to consummate her marriage vows.

(2) *By the clear and unmistakable statement by the angel of the conception and birth of the Son, Jesus, verse 31.*

The words of verse 31 are so like the prophet's words in Isaiah 7:14, that no one can fail to see the connection between the two passages. In the clearest and simplest way, the angel Gabriel instructed Mary as to God's intent about her, just as the prophet had spoken long before. Three brief clauses say it all. Mary shall conceive, she shall give birth to a son, and the son's name shall be "Jesus" (*Immanuel* in Isaiah 7:14). "Immanuel" means that the son born of the virgin was God Himself manifest in flesh—"God with us," while the name "Jesus" denotes that He would save us from our sins. The future tenses of the verbs are not expressive of mere desire, but are futuristic and prophetic. All these events would take place; they would occur without any question. The words of the angel could be spoken with such positiveness and certainty because the divine decree and purpose in accord with the divine foreknowledge could not possibly fail. And note, there is not one word about Joseph as the father of this son whom Mary was to bear, but only the mention of the Lord God, and of the son's personal name—Jesus!

(3) *By the fact that upon the basis of her own words, Mary had never known a man.*

In verse 34, Mary's response to the angel's announcement is recorded by inspiration. Her response did not indicate unbelief on her part. She did not doubt what the angel said. She was, in a way, like Nicodemus, who also asked "how" about the new birth. What perplexed Mary was not that what God said would not come to pass but that she was to have a son, not at a distant time after her marriage to Joseph, but as she properly judged, even before she and Joseph came together. With this "how," she asked for an explanation, and "since" expressed her reason for perplexity—that is, *she had not known a man.* Hence, she desired to know how this announcement could be consistent with her conscious virginity. Mary could only understand the conceiving and bearing a son as being possible by sexual union with her husband, the universal natural law of procreation. She did not disbelieve, she was not doubting, she was entirely willing to bear the great son of whom the angel had spoken to her, but what about the husband from whom she was to conceive that son? With her marriage still not consummated, how was she, a virgin maiden, to have a son? For up to the point of Mary's question, the angel had intimated nothing whatever about how she would be made the mother of such a son.

(4) *By the angel's announcement that the miraculous conception of a son in her virgin's womb would be done by the power of the Holy Spirit of God.*

The angel's answer to Mary's question is recorded in verse 35. There is no rebuke given to Mary as though there was an impropriety in her asking. In fact, as Lenski states:

> It seems as if the angel purposely left out this vital point in his announcement, thus inducing Mary's question, in order to state this point more emphatically, for it is absolutely essential in the proper conception of Mary's son, our Saviour. . . . The conception was a miracle, and all who reject miracles will find some way to rid themselves of the angel's words. All who want a Saviour without deity will do the same. A son conceived by Mary from Joseph, conceived before their marriage was consummated, or a bastard conceived from somebody else is more to their liking than God's Son born of the virgin Mary. Two things are certain: the texts of Matthew and Luke still stand, and the sense of what they record also stands; all efforts to the contrary only make these facts stand out the more.[1]

---

1 R.C.H. Lenski, *The Interpretation of Luke,* (Columbus, Ohio: Lutheran Book Concern, 1934), p. 526.

Note that the angel said: "The Holy Spirit shall come upon thee, and the power of the Highest shall overshadow thee." This is as far as revelation can take the miracle because the human mind is not able to follow beyond this. But the essential point is clear: the conception in the womb of the virgin Mary was caused by the third Person of the Godhead, the Holy Spirit. He did not operate from a distance, nor did He perform His work through another intermediary. He Himself came upon Mary; He Himself worked the conception by His own almighty power. Luke states that the power of the Highest "overshadowed" Mary. The verb is *episkiasei,* which means "to envelop in shadow" as a shining cloud surrounds and envelops one with brightness. In Luke 1:35, it is descriptive of the Holy Spirit exerting creative energy upon the womb of the virgin Mary to bring about the miraculous conception of the son Jesus. The entire conception was wrought by the omnipotent operation of the Holy Spirit of God. The purport of the whole account is that the beginning of that supernatural life of which Mary was to be the mother, would be wrought by the direct agency of the eternal God Himself, Mary being still and remaining, so far as this birth was concerned, an unsullied virgin. The inspired record presents the fact, and the fact stands.

Now, note what the RSV and NEB have done with this testimony of Luke. For one thing, they have taken the question of Mary in verse 34, and changed it so that it reads: "How can this be, *since*

I have no husband?" Anyone can see that there is an enormous difference between these two translations: "since I have no husband" (RSV, NEB), and "seeing I know not a man" (KJV). It is sad but true that a good many young women have become mothers of children when actually they had no husbands. But, as Dr. McClain points out, "In all the history of the world, no woman save Mary alone, ever bore a child when she had not previously known a man."[1]

The RSV and NEB translations are totally wrong. The Greek text simply does not read that way. What Mary *did* say was: "I know not a man" —*epei andra ou' ginosko*. The verb *ginosko* does not mean "have," and is never rendered so in the New Testament. It means "know," and in Luke 1:34, it has the sense of "know carnally in sexual experience." There is no possible way in which the revisers could translate the clause as they have done except to deliberately read their rendering into the sentence. They may call their translation an "idiomatic expression," but if so, it is the most extraordinary idiomatic expression in all the history of languages. A true idiomatic expression still does not divorce itself from the original meaning of the passage of Scripture. The translators of the RSV and NEB had no grammatical basis to make the change, and to make it appear that Mary said some-

---

1 Alva J. McClain, op. cit., p. 140.

thing she did not say. The Greek text speaks for itself.

8. THE PROPHECY IN ISAIAH 7:14 WAS SPECIFICALLY GIVEN AS A SIGN TO THE HOUSE OF DAVID.

According to the immediately preceding context of the prophecy, Ahaz, King of Judah, was told to ask for *a sign* from the Lord "either in the depth, or in the height above" (v. 11). But Ahaz declined on a pretense of piety (v. 12), and the Lord turned His address to the House of David: "Hear ye now, O house of David.... Therefore the Lord Himself shall give you *a sign*: Behold, the virgin [*ha-almah*] shall conceive and bear a son..." (vv. 13, 14). Some interpreters have made the *almah* to be the wife of the prophet Isaiah (see 8:1-4); others have said that the almah is the wife of Ahaz, so that the promised son is Hezekiah; and of course a third interpretation abandons all such identifications, and holds that merely a "young woman" is intended, which is the position of the liberal theologians and critics of the doctrine of the Virgin Birth.

But how could any of the interpretations be true which find in this miraculous conception and childbearing of the *almah* only an ordinary birth? Why should an ordinary birth be regarded as *a sign* to the House of David? Or to anyone else? Certainly no natural birth could possibly have served any purpose as *a sign*. The birth of a son to some young Jewish woman through sexual union with her husband could have no special significance. The

Church Father Justin Martyr, in his dialogue with Trypho, in the middle of the second century, said:

> For if this one was to be born of the union between the sexes, as all the other first-born sons are born, why did God say that He would produce a sign, which is not common to all first-born? But anticipating through the Holy Spirit that which is truly a sign and was destined, to be sure, for the race of men—that is, that the first-born of all created things should by incarnation through a virgin's womb truly become a child—He proclaimed it aforehand in one and another fashion (as I have set forth to you), in order that when it happened it might appear to have happened by the power and purpose of the Maker of all things.[1]

Dr. Machen, commenting on the statement by the Church Father Justin Martyr, wrote:

> No doubt this argument may have to be supplemented in the light of subsequent investigation, but whether it has really been invalidated may be seriously doubted....[2]

Another noted Church Father of the second century, Irenaeus, wrote concerning Isaiah 7:14:

> For what great thing or what sign should have been in this, that a young woman conceiving by a man should bring forth—a thing which happens to all women that produce offspring? But since an unlooked for salvation was to be provided through the help of God, so also was the un-

---

1 Justin Martyr, *Dialogues with Trypho;* Dialogue, 84, quoted in *The Virgin Birth of Christ*, by J. Gresham Machen. p. 291.
2 Machen, op. cit., p. 291.

looked for birth from a virgin accomplished.[1]

Commenting on the matter of the sign and the critical attitude toward *almah,* Dr. McClain has written:

> Finally, on the assumption accepted by the destructive critics, namely, that the *almah* of Isaiah 7:14 was not a *virgin* but only a *young woman,* who in the days of the prophet bore a child by natural generation of a human father, it is difficult to see how this event could possibly have been any kind of a "sign" of unusual significance to the House of David. The words of Isaiah 7:11 indicate that the "sign" to be given by the Lord Himself would be something beyond and above anything in the ordinary world. How could such a sign be fulfilled by the birth of a child as the result of a man and a woman coming together? One might argue, with some justification, it would be a much greater sign *if no child* were conceived and born in such an event.[2]

The word *almah* stands as it was written into the inspired record by the prophet hundreds of years ago. It is the word of the Holy Spirit who gave it to Isaiah, the same Holy Spirit who then later, according to the divine plan, came upon the *almah* to bring about the miraculous conception and birth. The *sign* is not that some young woman would conceive in a natural way and bear a son. Rather it is that the virgin (*ha-almah*), the specific virgin to

---

1 The Quarterly Record, *Trinitarian Bible Society,* (London, England), April-June Issue, 1970, p. 9.

2 McClain, op. cit., p. 139.

whom also Micah 5:3 refers and Matthew and Luke positively identify would conceive a son by the power of the Holy Spirit of God, before she and her husband had ever come together. He would be the holy Son of God, who by this virgin birth became "Immanuel." The fulfillment of this great sign is the Virgin Birth and incarnation of our Lord Jesus Christ, "and without controversy great is the mystery of godliness: God was manifest in the flesh..." (1 Tim. 3:16a). And all true believers will confess—must confess—their personal belief in this great and essential doctrinal truth (1 John 4:1-3).

It is not only the use of this one significant word in Isaiah 7:14 which leads us to expect the miraculous in that which the prophet proceeds to announce. The whole passage is couched in such terms as to create in the believer's heart a sense of profound mystery and of the miraculous, of the supernatural activity of the eternal God. Machen states:

> It is certainly clear that something more than the Israelitish people is meant by the figure of the "Servant of Jehovah" in the latter part of Isaiah; and it is certainly clear that something more is meant by "Immanuel" in our passage than the child of the prophet, or of Ahaz, or of any ordinary young woman of that time. A really sympathetic and intelligent reader can hardly, we think, doubt but that in the "Immanuel" of the seventh and eighth chapters of Isaiah, in the "child" of the ninth chapter, whose name shall be called "wonderful, counsellor, mighty God, everlasting Father, Prince of Peace," in the "branch" of the eleventh chapter—*one mighty,*

divine personage is meant. The common minimizing interpretations may seem plausible in detail, but they disappear before the majestic sweep of the passages taken as a whole.[1]

A further point should be added. The word "sign" is a highly significant term in the Hebrew. It is the word which indicated the death of Eli's two sons in 1 Samuel 2:34; it designated the prophet Ezekiel himself as a sign to the House of Israel in Ezekiel 24:24; and it is the word which described the Sabbath as a bond between God and His people in Exodus 31:13. It has but three letters, and is spelled *'oth*. While too much credence is often given to numerics in the Scriptures, the fact remains that the Hebrew term for "sign" contains but three letters, and the number "3" is the number representing the Holy Trinity, the eternal Godhead. This prophecy in Isaiah 7:14 has the divine stamp upon it; it is a specific and supernatural revelation carrying the trinitarian signature. It is the word from the Lord God Himself concerning the *almah,* through whom God should be with us, by means of which God was manifest in flesh.

It is also an extraordinary fact that the first and last letters of the word "sign" (*'oth*), are *aleph* and *tau,* the first and last letters of the Hebrew alphabet. This is certainly no mere coincidence, and should immediately direct our thoughts to the statement of the Lord Himself, recorded in Revelation 1:6, 11, "I am Alpha and Omega, the first

---

1 Machen, op. cit., p. 292.

and the last...." The "Alpha" and "Omega," mentioned also in Revelation 21:6 and 22:13, are the first and last letters of the Greek alphabet. As the Lord of Glory is the "Alpha" and "Omega" of the Greek alphabet, He is also the "Aleph" and "Tau" of the Hebrew alphabet. He is the first and last, the beginning and ending in both. He is God's supreme revelation from the first to the last letter, the God of all history from start to finish, all God's saving work from origination to consummation. He is "Immanuel," the holy Son of God, the only-begotten One, born of the *almah,* Mary, the handmaid of the Lord.

Such is the evidence for the translation and meaning of the Hebrew word *almah* as "virgin." If this evidence is rejected, then the inspiration of the Holy Scriptures is denied and their authority rejected. The Virgin Birth is an integral part of the Biblical testimony concerning the Lord Jesus Christ. It is thus absolutely essential to the true Christian faith. Therefore it is necessary for the corporate witness of the Church, and is basic for the personal testimony of every true child of God. The Gospel which we believe and proclaim is centered in the Person and work of the One who came into the world by means of the miracle in the virgin's womb. And the New Testament records the fulfillment of the great event prophetically set forth in Isaiah 7:14. As Dr. Machen states:

The New Testament presentation of Jesus Christ is not an agglomeration, but an organism, and of that organism the virgin birth is an integral part. Remove the part, and the whole becomes harder and not easier to accept; the New Testament account of Jesus is most convincing when it is taken as a whole. Only one Jesus is presented in the Word of God; and that Jesus did not come into the world by ordinary generation, but was conceived in the womb of the virgin (*ha-almah*), by the Holy Spirit.[1]

---

[1] Machen, op. cit., p. 397.
The parenthesis in the last line of the quotation is mine.

Part Two

I

Excursus on the Importance of the Virgin Birth

The essential nature and significance of the doctrine of the Virgin Birth should always occupy a prominent place in our thinking. Its vital importance to the historic Christian faith may be expressed in the following six propositions.

1. THE TRUSTWORTHINESS OF THE GOSPEL RECORDS IS DEPENDENT UPON THE TRUTH OF THE VIRGIN BIRTH.

There is no doubt that the Virgin Birth of Christ is a favorite point of attack by the liberal critics. It has become so because the Virgin Birth is to them apparently a vulnerable ground. If the critical scholars can discredit the Virgin Birth, it means that the Gospel writers, Matthew and Luke, are either guilty of willful falsification or victims of blind credulity. The Virgin Birth statement in these two Gospel accounts can be successfully assailed upon no other basis which does not involve Matthew and Luke in such charges. Should the liberal theologians be correct in their attack upon the Virgin Birth, it necessarily follows that everything in the writings of Matthew and Luke is open to question, and we cannot rely upon anything they wrote. If the Virgin Birth accounts in Matthew and Luke are fable, invention, legend, and fabrication, to which no credit can be attached, then everything else in those Gospel narratives is equally dubious and untrustworthy. It is upon the truth of these Gospel records that our belief in the Virgin Birth depends. If these cannot be trusted we are left with no real ground for our faith.

However, the critical attack against the miracle of the Virgin Birth, formidable and malicious as it is, fails to accomplish its purpose in the light of the evidence. The proof for the genuineness of the Gospels of Matthew and Luke is convincing, and the narrative accounts of the Virgin Birth in the two Gospels are undoubtedly genuine parts of their respective Gospels. The manuscript evidence of this is overwhelming. Moreover, the two accounts are independent, that is, one is not derived from the other. Yet they both attest in clear detail that Jesus Christ was conceived by the power of the Holy Spirit in the womb of the virgin, Mary of Nazareth, who was espoused to Joseph, whose wife she afterward became.

But even more convincing and assuring is the fact that the narrative accounts of the Virgin Birth in Matthew and Luke do not stand alone. For there is a great mass of convergent testimony in the Gospel records and the rest of the New Testament to the supernatural person and work of Jesus Christ. Particularly is this true with respect to the supreme miracle of the resurrection. The proofs that the Lord rose from the dead after three days and three nights in the tomb are indeed convincing and incontrovertible. And if the supernatural is accepted at any one point, there is no reason why it cannot be accepted at all other points, particularly in connection with the Virgin Birth. Having once concluded that Jesus Christ is a supernatural person, and that the Gospel accounts of Him are not myth or fancy of the early Church, we shall have no difficulty in accepting the fact that He was supernaturally conceived in the virgin's womb. The narratives of the Virgin Birth in Matthew and Luke are completely congruous with the whole New Testament account of Christ. And if it is true that Christ actually rose bodily from the dead—and it is—and if He really is the kind of person depicted in the New Testament—and He is—then there is every reason to believe that He was conceived by the Holy Spirit, and born of the virgin Mary.

2. THE FACT OF THE VIRGIN BIRTH IS IMPORTANT BECAUSE IT INVOLVES THE WHOLE DOCTRINE OF THE INCARNATION.

The doctrine of the Virgin Birth provides the only logical explanation of the entrance of the eternal Son of God into human flesh, form, and nature. It is the one reasonable and responsible answer as to how Christ entered into the world. The Gnostics insisted that the Son of God united with the man Jesus at the baptism. It was suggested that the man Jesus was received up gradually into union with the eternal Son. But such theories deprive us of the full doctrine of the incarnation and its blessedness and assurance to our souls. It was essential that the Son of God should enter the world and live a complete human life upon the earth. Yet the human life of the Son would not be complete unless it began in the mother's womb. The incarnation cannot therefore be fixed at a later time than at the moment when the babe was conceived. Then and there is to be found the stupendous event when the eternal Son of God assumed our nature, becoming true man so that from that point on, He was and is both God and man.

It has also been advocated that it is far more reasonable to assume that Christ entered the world in the ordinary manner by simply being born of two parents. Liberalism tells us glibly that there is nothing wrong with such a view. Joseph and Mary were espoused, and there is nothing unholy about human parentage. It is a sacred institution of God's own decree. Why then should we hesitate to admit that Jesus was born by ordinary human generation of two parents?

But the very opposite is true. The natural result of the ordinary process of procreation from human parentage is the beginning of a new personality, the birth of a new child. However, Jesus Christ was the pre-existent Son of God. He did not receive His personality through human birth, for He was a person before His birth. Hence, there was no need for the ordinary process of procreation. Such a process would have been completely out of the question. As Dr. McClain has written:

> The use of the ordinary procreative process would have necessitated a special miracle to prevent the production of a wholly new personality, distinct from the personality of the Son of God. Those who accept the pre-existence of Jesus Christ as a personal being must also accept some kind of a miracle in bringing Him into human life with a vital connection with the human race. The miracle of the virgin birth is by far the most reasonable. By a special creative act, the personality of the eternal Son is clothed with human nature in the womb of the virgin Mary.[1]

And Machen writes:

> In the overwhelming majority of cases those who reject the virgin birth reject the whole supernatural view of Christ. They often profess belief in the "incarnation," but the word is apt to mean to them almost the exact opposite of what the New Testament means when it says that "the Word became flesh." To these modern men, the

---

1 Dr. Alva J. McClain, *Unpublished Notes in Theology*, (Winona Lake, Indiana: Grace Theological Seminary, 1941), p. 38.

incarnation means that God and man are one. To the New Testament it means rather that they are not mixed in one, but that the eternal Son of God became man, assumed our nature, by a stupendous miracle, to redeem us from sin. Seldom indeed does any real belief in the incarnation go along with a rejection of the miracle of the virgin birth.[1]

3. THE VIRGIN BIRTH IS ESSENTIAL TO THE SINLESS HUMAN NATURE OF CHRIST.

The Scriptures clearly teach that the whole race of mankind is under the awful curse of sin and death. Every man born into this world is born with a sinful nature which is capable of the worst sins. It is universally true that sinful humanity, in the ordinary course of procreation, reproduces its own sinful nature. The Lord Jesus Christ said to Nicodemus: "That which is born of flesh is flesh" (John 3:6a). Yet here is the amazing phenomenon of One who came into the world and lived an absolutely sinless life in the midst of a sinful humanity. A sinless man is perhaps a greater miracle in the moral realm than the Virgin Birth in the physical realm. But the testimony of Scripture stands, and the evidences are convincing. However the enemies of the Gospel may seek to disprove the sinless human life of the Lord, nevertheless the facts abide. Christ frequently went up to the temple, but He never offered sacrifices. He prayed constantly, but never

---

1 Machen, op. cit., p. 391.

sought forgiveness for Himself. He taught that all men need the new birth, but His words indicated that He Himself had no such need. The Lord challenged all His critics and His enemies to convict Him of a single sin. He was indeed sinless, as His whole life demonstrated, but when, in all the expanse of time, has natural generation ever given birth to a sinless personality?

The sinlessness of our Lord's human life cannot be separated from the fact of His virgin birth. If there is a moral taint in the human race, if in the very blood and constitution of humanity there is the ineradicable disposition to sin, then it is totally inconceivable that anyone born by natural generation should escape the sinfulness of that race. If Jesus Christ was born by ordinary procreation, of two sinful parents, He could not possibly have been without sin. But the birth of Christ was not an ordinary birth, by natural means, as is common to all others of the race. It was a divine person who already existed, entering into a new mode of existence. Miracle alone could produce such a wonder. What took place was a divine, creative miracle wrought in the womb of the virgin Mary—conceived by the Holy Spirit of God—which made certain total freedom from the slightest taint of sin. The sinless, supernatural life of the Son of God on earth requires the Virgin Birth at the beginning. How, except by virgin birth, could the Lord have lived a complete and sinless life from the mother's womb, and yet have been from the very beginning no product of what had gone before, but a supernatural person come down from heaven into the world to save sinners from their sins?

4. The Virgin Birth is absolutely essential to every other point in the doctrine of Christ.

The Biblical testimony with relation to Christ comprises a line of doctrinal truth which extends from His pre-existence to His second coming. He who was born at Bethlehem existed before there ever was a town of Bethlehem. Historically, His pre-existence is revealed first, but the study of His pre-existence brings us inevitably to His deity. Yet while He was true God, He was also true man. The Son of God was incarnate in flesh and dwelt among men, yet without sin. He went to the cross, and having died for the ungodly, to save sinners from their sins, He rose from the dead and showed Himself living to His apostles by many incontrovertible proofs. After spending forty post-resurrection days with His apostles, instructing them of the things pertaining to the kingdom of God, He ascended into glory, back to the place from whence He had come. His own particular promise to return was confirmed by the angels at the scene of the ascension. Such is the line of doctrine concerning the Lord Jesus Christ, established by the Scriptures, to which we must faithfully hold, and for which we must earnestly contend.

Certain critics, however, insist that we are trying to maintain too long a battle front. We must shorten the line by giving up certain parts of that line, which are not essential to the Christian faith—such as the Virgin Birth. But such a concession is impossible. We cannot dispense with the Virgin Birth without giving up all along the line. We cannot surrender the Virgin Birth without surrendering every other point of the doctrine of Christ. If we yield to critical pressure in the matter of the Virgin Birth, then our whole doctrinal position is in jeopardy. For one born of human parents by the ordinary procreative process could not possibly have been pre-existent. If Christ was not virgin-born, then He cannot be God, and if He is not God, then He is the greatest impostor the world has ever seen, in leading men to worship and trust Him. His death on the cross might have been tragic, heroic indeed —the noble sacrifice of one who died for the truth He held—but it was not the vicarious, substitutionary death of the Savior, who thereby wrought redemption for mankind. If He was not the pre-existent Son of God, incarnate in human flesh, but mere man then He is still dead, and could not have risen from the dead as the Scriptures testify. It would have been impossible for His apostles to have seen Him after His death and burial, and His ascension was the creation of their pathological fancy.

However, we believe the great doctrinal facts concerning Christ because they *are* facts. We believe that He is God manifest in the flesh to take away our sins because He *is* God manifest in flesh. We believe in His sinless human life because the fact is that His human life on earth *was* without sin. We believe that He died on the cross, was buried, and then rose from the dead after three days and three nights, because He *did* so die and He *did* rise out of death. Everything about our Lord Jesus Christ was supernatural. He was a supernatural person with supernatural knowledge and power. He performed supernatural works, lived a supernatural life, and proclaimed a supernatural message. He died a supernatural death, He rose from the dead in a supernatural manner, and He went back to the glory supernaturally. When He comes again, it will be a great and blessed supernatural event. In view of all this, how is it possible that such a person as the Lord of glory could have entered the world by natural generation? The Virgin Birth is absolutely necessary to complete the record of the doctrine of Christ.

5. THE VIRGIN BIRTH IS VITALLY RELATED TO THE INFALLIBILITY AND AUTHORITY OF SCRIPTURE.

There is no doubt that the New Testament teaches the Virgin Birth of Christ. Anyone can read the record which describes Jesus Christ as having been conceived by the Holy Spirit of God and born of the virgin Mary. The critical question raised is that whether in making such an assertion the record is true or false. If the Scripture is regarded as being wrong in what it says concerning the Virgin Birth of Christ, then obviously it is neither infallible nor authoritative.

Modern liberalism maintains that no matter what the Bible says about the birth of Christ without a human father, it may still be accepted as authoritative in the sphere of religion. Irrespective of the manner of the Lord's birth, and the real meaning of His death and His alleged resurrection, we may still follow Christ and experience His presence in our souls. Salvation does not rest upon musty old records purporting to tell what may or may not have actually occurred so long ago. Salvation is independent of history and depends only upon what is with us here and now. Give us the teaching and example of Jesus, and we have all that is needed no matter how He might have been born into the world. What does this matter anyway? We find our God here and now in the depths of our own souls. Virgin Birth or no Virgin Birth, it is the teaching of Jesus that stirs us and leads us out into the living of a good life. Such a life is entirely possible independent of events such as the Virgin Birth. It is the life of Christ that holds meaning for us, and the spirit of His life has been handed down from generation to generation. To catch that spirit, we do not have to hold any particular view about Christ and His birth. This kind of religion is founded upon the ability of man to save himself apart from the historic facts of the Gospel. Those who hold to such a notion are not greatly interested in the fact of the Virgin Birth.

The *true* Christian faith however is founded upon a factual account of events that took place in history, in the external world of men. The Bible writers have recorded these things in an orderly and trustworthy manner. An essential part of that record is the fact that the Lord Jesus Christ was conceived by the Holy Spirit, and born of the virgin Mary. If this great fact is rejected as being untrue, then the testimony of all the Gospel writers, and the testimony of all the New Testament, are also untrue. If indeed, the Virgin Birth is rejected, then the infallibility of Scripture and the authority of the Bible are to be cast aside. Even if we should continue to rest for salvation upon parts of the Biblical record, but reject other parts, our belief in the infallibility and authority of the Scriptures would be gone and our faith would be in vain. We might still hold that many of the things which are recorded in the Bible are true, but we could no longer rely upon the Bible as such, and the doctrine of the infallibility of Scripture would have to to be abandoned.

Hence the infallibility and authority of the Scriptures are essentially involved in the matter of the Virgin Birth of Christ. The Bible clearly teaches the Virgin Birth, and those who accept this teaching and believe in the Virgin Birth, may continue with all certainty and trust, to hold to the full and absolute truthfulness of the Bible. Since the blessed Lord was really born into the world without a human father, then such was God's own inimitable way for the Son to enter the world. It was therefore the best way, and the only way, and any other way would have been wrong. It is extremely important for believers to have the record of the Virgin Birth, and to know the facts of that record. If the New Testament did not give to us the inspired testimony of the Virgin Birth, our knowledge of the Lord Jesus Christ would be significantly and irreparably impoverished, and there would be a fatal defection in the Biblical view of Christ.

6. THE VIRGIN BIRTH IS A NECESSARY PART OF THE TRUE CHRISTIAN CONFESSION.

The question has been asked, "Is it necessary for a man to believe in the Virgin Birth if he is to become a true Christian? Is the knowledge of this doctrine essential for saving faith?" Perhaps the question is not appropriately put when it is asked in this manner, for who is able to tell exactly how much knowledge of the facts about Christ is necessary to a man's possession of saving faith? How can we say that full knowledge and conviction are necessary before a man can place his trust in Christ for salvation? What right do we have to assert that unless a man has come to full knowledge and conviction concerning the miracle of the Virgin Birth recorded in Matthew and Luke, he cannot be saved? Some knowledge is required, but only God knows exactly how much is necessary. God alone can tell what convictions are needed to open the human heart to the truth of the Gospel. It is doubtless true that one can be saved without any conscious knowledge and conviction concerning the fact of the Virgin Birth. Certainly when we sit down to talk to an unbeliever about the salvation of his soul, we will not engage in a theological discussion of the Virgin Birth. Unsaved men need to know that they are dead in trespasses and sins, but that God has provided a way of life which is bestowed through simple but genuine faith in the Savior. Still, saving faith is the reception of the Lord Jesus Christ as He is offered to mankind in the Gospel. And an integral part of that good news of salvation for lost men is the blessed fact that Christ came into the world by the miracle of Virgin Birth. "Forasmuch then as the children are partakers of flesh and blood, he also himself likewise took part of the same..." (Heb. 2:14). "And ye know that he was manifested to take away our sins..." (1 John 3:5). The nature of His appearance in the world of men to deal with sin was by incarnation, the portal of which was the Virgin Birth. It must ever be kept in mind that the Virgin Birth is a vitally essential part of the entire New Testament witness concerning Christ and that witness must be taken as it stands.

One thing is certain, while belief in the Virgin Birth may not be necessary to a man's salvation, it is most assuredly necessary to the true Christian faith. Even if a man may be brought to saving faith without knowledge of the reality of the Virgin Birth, it is incredible to think that it is possible to be saved while knowingly denying the doctrine. We consent to a logical order for the proofs of Christianity, in which order the doctrine of the Virgin Birth would not come first. The atoning death, burial, and resurrection of Christ constitute the heart of the Gospel message, and it is to these facts that the person who needs to be saved should be directed first. Nevertheless in the matter of vital doctrine, the Scripture sets forth a final test for true Christian belief. In 1 John 4:2-3 (LT), it is written: "By this know ye the Spirit of God: every spirit that confesseth that Jesus Christ has come in the flesh is of God; And every spirit that confesseth not (that) Jesus (Christ has come) is not of God...." As John under inspiration presents it, to deny the complete reality of the Virgin Birth and Incarnation is to strike at the very foundation of the true Christian faith. This is the test to be applied. Examine a man's confession; if he holds to the Virgin Birth and Incarnation, he is truly of God. If he does not believe this, then he is not of God. True indeed, we cannot read a man's heart. But the Holy Spirit has given us the one safe test —the man's confession. One confesses not only with his lips, but also with his practice of life, hence we must examine both. Still, the absence of the oral confession of the Virgin Birth, or an erroneous confession of it, will be exposed in the life. The "mystery of godliness," God manifest in the flesh (1 Tim. 3:16), is the vital point in the true confession of Christ. The true, eternal, almighty God became incarnate in human flesh, form, and nature, by means of the Virgin Birth, to save us from our sins. Every genuine child of God will meet the test, and make this confession with confidence and conviction. It is here that we stand: this is the great fundamental of the faith, the eternal God-Man, the divine-human Person of Jesus Christ the Son of God Who came first to redeem us and is coming again to receive us.

II

Excursus on the Dangers of Denying the Virgin Birth and Incarnation

"Beloved, do not believe every spirit, but test the spirits whether they are from God; because many false prophets have gone out into the world. In this know ye the Spirit of God: every spirit that confesseth Jesus Christ having come in flesh is from God; And every spirit that confesseth not Jesus (having come in flesh) is not from God; and this is that spirit of antichrist, of which ye have heard that it should come, and even now already is it in the world" (1 John 4:1-3—LT).

The great personal Source, from Whom we know that God is in us, and that our believing faith in Christ is real is the Holy Spirit (1 John 3:23-24). From Him comes the conviction and assurance that we are of the truth, and He speaks to us and in us through the Word. This Holy Spirit Who resides in us, and imparts to us the confidence of the divine presence, also provides the wisdom and discernment which enable us to put to the test those men who are religious teachers and prophets abroad in the world. From the Spirit comes the knowledge of our relationship to the Lord, and from the same Spirit, as He teaches us in the Word, come the warnings as to false prophets and teachers of religious error.

The Johannine Epistles show clearly how greatly John was pressed in mind and heart for the people of God in that day of surging early church activity and the prevalence of supernatural phenomena. Simple, gullible souls were so impressed by things they saw and heard, as to be dazzled and completely taken in by them. (Cf. the earlier ministry of Simon Magus in Samaria, and its astounding effects, Acts 8:9-11.) Many believers in those days had begun to accept uncritically all teaching which seemed to be given under inspiration, and therefore apparently from God. Hence, it was imperative that Christians be warned that there were many false teachers at work in the world and among the churches. A simple but decisive test must be laid down, by which all religious teachers were to be measured. These men were to be tested out as to their confession of faith. If they confessed that the Son of God, Jesus Christ, had come in the flesh they were genuine, teachers of the truth, and therefore to be trusted. By this, the Spirit of God would be known.

Anyone who denied the Virgin Birth and Incarnation of the Son of God was not of God.

Today there are many false teachers in the modern world and many voices clamoring for attention and claiming to be the spokesmen for Christianity. Yet these deny, in one way or another, the fact that the Son of God has come in the flesh. Christendom is saturated with liberal theology, unitarianism, neo-orthodoxy, universalism, the love theology of situation ethics, and all shades and hues of materialistic philosophy, radicalism, secularized religion, cultic superstition and idolatry. All of these are a part of the great ecumenical pantheon which rejects the Lord Jesus Christ as the revelation absolute of the eternal God. These deny that He came into the world by any other means than ordinary, human procreation. Therefore, believers have this word of warning from God, sent through John, that caution must be exercised in accepting the message of today's religious teachers and leaders. There is far too much misguided charity and undue tolerance toward false teachers and their false teachings in our time. And there is far too great an ignorance prevailing among believers with regard to the rapidly mounting scope and influence of the ecumenical apostasy, and the related dreadful increase of the evil activity of the spirit of lawlessness (2 Thess. 2:7a). The people of God need to be discerning toward *the character* of the message being taught, whether it is genuine or spurious, but also toward *its origin,* whether divine or diabolical. The saints

81

must be able to *know* and *identify* what they hear and read, and not be credulous: "Be not believing every spirit..." (1 John 4:1—LT).

The *attitude* of believers toward religious teachers is designated by John as being twofold. *First,* we are not to believe them all. In 3:23, we are taught the commandment of God "that we should believe on the name of His Son Jesus Christ...." In 4:1, John develops this term "believe." He relates it to all human teachers who claim to be spiritual leaders who speak from God, and specifies the test to be applied to them. Some people believe everything they hear if it has a plausible sound. They take it in and delight in it without even so much as applying a single test. But the true Christian faith is not disposed to credulity. True faith examines its object before placing trust and confidence in it. Nothing should be received hastily, but everything should be subjected to calm consideration and severe searching. First Thessalonians 5:21 tells us to put all things to the test and hold fast that which is good. John says (LT): "Do not be placing your confidence and trust in what every man who calls himself a prophet of God, or spiritual leader, who claims to be bringing you the Word of God, preaches and teaches and asks you to believe." Christians are to exercise their own God-given faculties in this matter, as indwelt by the Holy Spirit of God, with the Word itself as the guide, and not to let somebody else do it for them.

Second, we are to put a test to these religious

teachers. John writes: "Do not be believing every spirit, but always be testing them out" (1 John 4:1 —LT). The object of this testing is to determine whether these religious teachers are from God (*ek tou Theou*). This test will penetrate any deception, and will expose falsity, showing whether the teachers and their teaching have their origin, being, power, and incentive in God, or in some ungodly, antichristian source. It is vitally essential for us to know whether these religious leaders, with what is in their hearts, are really from God. We must determine whether they are called and sent by Him, or if they are masquerading agents of the evil one. If they are from God, we may receive their message and lay it to heart. If they are not from God, their message is full of deadly poison, and we must reject it and stand against it, helping others to resist it. The testing is a continuous thing—it must not cease. We must always be putting these men and their message to the test. There is no time when we can afford to be off our guard. Note also that all believers are here instructed to do the testing. This is not something that is reserved by God for ministers of the gospel. It is true that men are given as guides, teachers, pastors, and leaders and all true servants of the Lord will keep their people instructed and informed in all matters pertaining to false teaching and apostasy (1 Tim. 4:1-6). In fact, John himself is offering such trained, mature, wise counsel in this passage. But all Christians are to make the test for themselves. They are to keep on making it, always

83

becoming more proficient at it and aiding others in doing it properly, for the world is full of counterfeit "Christian" teachers.

The *assessment* of these teachers is significantly recorded in the last clause of verse 1. As to *person*, they are men. There is no thought here of "spirit" (*pneuma*), and "spirits" (*pneumata*), as designating the inner part of a human being, which together with the soul (*psuchei*) makes one a personal being, as Paul speaks of body, soul, and spirit, in 1 Thessalonians 5:23. Neither is John speaking of some kind of supernatural spirit, which roams about, communicating with all who will lend themselves to such influences. These "spirits" are *men*, as such, with their inner spiritual character. They are men whose spirit and nature are derived from the great evil spirit himself, Satan (John 8:44). As to *position*, they are false prophets (*pseudopropheitai*). This is definite identification of the spirits as *men*. Moreover, they have assumed the place of prophets for themselves, since they are not called by God as *His* prophets. They appear to be genuine; they are religious; they make predictions and prognostications; and they speak grandiose things. But they are false (*pseudo*). They pretend to have the Spirit of God, to be moved and directed by Him. They claim to bring the truth to men, while they do nothing of the kind. Their intent is to deceive believers, and lead them off into divergent paths of confusion and disaster, where their faith will be wrecked, and their witness destroyed.

As to *place*, they are in the world, all around us.
The realm of their activity and ministry is thus
clearly defined. They are everywhere in this present
cosmos, many in conspicuous and influential posts,
and multitudes of others in lesser positions. They
are of the world, so they are at home in it, and
familiar with its ways. Moreover, the perfect tense
of the verb "have gone out" (*exeleiluthasin*) denotes a definite moving out into the world and remaining there (4:1). It shows how these teachers
have begun to circulate among men and continue
to do so in ever increasing numbers. The modernists and apostates are here to stay. Nothing can
push them out. Their ecumenical dream will even-
tually become a reality for a brief hour.

Having given these words of caution and warning, John proceeds in verses 2 and 3, to set forth
the divinely revealed means of detecting and dis-
tinguishing those teachers who are from God and
those who are not. The test is simply stated, but
its involvements are great. The confession of the
Virgin Birth and Incarnation of Jesus Christ the
Son of God is fundamental to a believer's walk and
witness. John states: "By (lit. 'in') this know ye
the Spirit of God..." (v. 2, New Scofield). In this
specific and particular respect, that is in connection
with the confession John is about to set forth in
the words that follow, the origin and character of
the teacher will be known. Here is the basis, or
touchstone, for sound testing. If the religious teacher
makes the confession here stated, then it will be

known that he has the Spirit of God, and what he says is true. But if the teacher, or prophet, does not make such a confession, then it will be known that he is not of God, and does not have the Spirit of God. This is the test that is to be applied.

The *avowal* of the confession appears in the words: "Every spirit that confesseth Jesus Christ having come in the flesh is of God" (LT). The *confession* itself is rendered by the verb *homologei,* which means "to say the same thing as another, and to declare it freely and openly." What the lips utter must correspond with the state of the heart. The two must be agreed. It is confessing with the voice the very thing which the heart holds and desires to make audible. The love of God has been poured out in the hearts of those who are true believers, through the Holy Spirit whom God has given to us. We thus have the Spirit in us, and it properly belongs to Him to confess in us and to us that Jesus Christ has come in the flesh. His confession *in* us and *to* us will be made known openly and boldly *through* us, since the matter is one of inward faith and outward witness. For there is no doubt that the inward spiritual character of the true confessor is derived from God and confirmed by the Holy Spirit. This confession is one which remains constant and consistent over the years as the present tense of the verb indicates. It carries on throughout a lifetime, enduring all the trials and tribulations of the earthly existence without succumbing to them.

The *content* of the confession must be noted with

care: "Jesus Christ having come in the flesh." Here is a great doctrinal statement which is the heart of the Christian confession. The verbal expression "is come" (KJV) is the Greek perfect participle *eleiluthota,* "having come" and should be so rendered. The English Versions translate: "that Jesus Christ is come in the flesh," making the participle read like a finite verb form, and the clause to appear as merely the recording of a fact. The true Christian not only admits the fact of Christ's Virgin Birth and Incarnation, but confesses *Jesus Christ Himself having come in flesh,* which means as Lord and Savior. And this can be truly done only by the Holy Spirit of God (1 Cor. 12:3). This confession identifies us with Him in His redemptive work, and as belonging to Him by virtue of that work. The Holy Spirit, confessing in us of His having come in the flesh makes us one with Him in this view of His coming: our guilt and condemnation now being His, and His taking our guilt and bearing our condemnation now being ours. His coming in flesh is His consenting to be crucified for us and to be then raised on account of our justification. The Holy Spirit in us, confessing Him as having come in flesh not only opens our lips to make this confession known to men, but opens to our hearts a prospect of hope and glory and the blessedness of the family-home in heaven. Having really come in flesh, and in the flesh having suffered for our sins, He raised the flesh in which He suffered and died to the supreme height and capacity for holy and happy being. The hope of Job was expressed by his words: "In my flesh shall I see God" (Job 19:26). And this is made certain by our Lord Jesus Christ having come in flesh, and through the Holy Spirit confessing in us that He has so come. The participle further shows the Son of God as having come *and remaining in the flesh*: the virgin-born Savior incarnate in human flesh, form, and nature, and continuing in that state. He is the God-Man in the glory, ready to return.

It is essential that we understand the full force and import of this confession. While the vital point is the frank and joyful acknowledgement of the Virgin Birth and Incarnation, it would be a serious mistake to think that the confession is limited to that one fact. For the believer's confession of the Virgin Birth and Incarnation of the Lord Jesus Christ is a confession of His pre-existence and deity. If He were merely a man, He could not have *come* in flesh—He would need *to be born* as any other man is born, by natural procreation, of two human parents. It is also a confession of the true humanity of Christ. He came *in the flesh*; and His coming in flesh brought Him, not merely into the position of one made under the law, but into the position, under the law, of those whose place He took. He was true man, although at no time did He cease to be God. It is moreover a confession of the Saviorhood of Christ. For Christ Jesus came into the world to save sinners; He was manifested to take away our sins, and *this required a body*. That body was prepared by special miraculous creation in the womb of the virgin and later offered on the cross once for all. This confession is finally a confession of the two real natures in the one ineffable person. He was and is true God and true Man, each, and both at once, the inexplicable but incontrovertible mystery of godliness. The confession, therefore, is not alone the confession of one great and vital truth in the doctrine of Christ, but veritably a confession of the whole of the Gospel.

The *absence* of the confession is then advanced by John as proof of unbelief: "And every spirit who does not confess Jesus (as having come in flesh) is not from God" (v. 3—LT). The expression "does not confess" (*mei homologei*) is actually stronger than the verbal "denies" would be and harmonizes with "is not from God." The name "Jesus" has the article of previous reference, and may be rendered "this," or "this one," that is this Jesus, in the full sense of all that the confession of verse 2 says about Him. Any denial of the Virgin Birth and Incarnation, or refusal to acknowledge that Christ has come in flesh, constitutes a denial of the whole doctrine of Christ, and of all that is characteristic of the Christian faith. And such denial is no less than "that (spirit) of antichrist, of which ye have heard that it would come, and now is already in the world" (LT).

In the mind of the Apostle John, the denial of "Jesus Christ having come in flesh" was to deny the whole redemptive work of Christ, and to strike at the very roots of true Christianity. To abandon this confession and to deny its great doctrinal truth is to manifest a total rejection of the Lord Jesus Christ. It is to deny both the supernatural coming of the Lord in human form and the grace which it reveals. Moreover, it exposes the grave dangers of unbelief and leads to certain definite and deadly consequences. Let us see what is involved in the denial of the great verity of Christ having come in the flesh.

1. THE DENIAL OF THE VIRGIN BIRTH AND INCARNATION IS TO DENY THE FACT THAT GOD HAS GIVEN AN EVERLASTING REVELATION OF HIMSELF IN BODILY FORM.

God is an invisible spirit, and the Scripture in John 1:18a testifies that "no man hath seen God at any time...." The innate curiosity and desire in the heart of man to see God and to know what He is like, are to be seen in the words of Philip, when he said to Christ: "Lord, show us the Father, and it sufficeth us" (John 14:8). But the eyes of sinful, mortal man could not bear the sight of God. Man could not stand before the deity and glory of God Almighty. The Lord said to Moses: "There shall no man see me and live" (Exod. 33:20). Man was created in the image of God, but did not remain true to the divine ideal. Man fell far from God by sin, and that image was defaced, marred, blurred and the soul lost. Hence, depravity and ruin were brought about and men built upon their fallen,

90

ruined nature a manifold false conception of God. In order to correct this—to draw the spirit of man back to the spiritual fact, to bring the heart of man to the knowledge of the true God, to reveal the eternal verities concerning Himself, to satisfy the need in the soul of man to see God and to know who and what He is—God sent His Son, perfect Man into the world. Thus John 1:18b (New Scofield) testifies: "The only begotten Son, who is in the bosom of the Father, he hath declared him." The verb, "hath declared" (*exeigeisato*), is of particular interest and importance. It is composed of *ek*, "out," and *heigeomai*, "lead." Hence it is "to lead out." The thought is that of leading out into clear view and comprehension. From this root we derive the English terms "exegesis, exegetical, exegete." The verb may be properly rendered "hath expounded," in the sense of "giving a full and detailed exposition and explanation." It is truly a choice word and is indeed expressive. The tense of the verb is the historical aorist, by which all that Christ "declared" concerning God is summed up, not only by His words and deeds, but by His very coming in flesh and the presence of His wonderful person. The Son is the full exegesis, the supreme exegete, the absolute interpreter of the eternal God. He is indeed "the image of the invisible God" (Col. 1:15a). John also records of Him that He said: "He that believeth in Me believeth not in Me, but in Him that sent Me. And he that seeth Me seeth Him that sent Me" (John 12:44, 45—LT). In the great final vision of the future redeemed humanity dwelling in the eternal city of God, the glory of God lights the city, and the Lamb is the lamp by which the light shines (Rev. 21:23).

To deny the fact of Jesus Christ having come in flesh is to deny that God has ever made Himself known except by signs and unusual events, and by natural theology. It is to reject the record of the Holy Scriptures and to hold them in contempt. It is to deny the very words of Christ Himself. It is to deny the great and blessed truth that He is the ever-lasting and absolute revelation of God in human flesh, form and nature, for the endless blessing of all who receive Him. It deprives men of the knowledge of who God is and what He is like, and leaves them with no other conception of Him than their own corrupted and perverted ideas, which are far from the truth. It abandons human beings to the deceptions and machinations of Satan the prince of this world-age, with no hope of deliverance and with no help from the sovereign God of the universe. It is to deny that there is a personal, living God in heaven who has not forsaken men in their sin and degradation, and who has not remained aloof and unknowable, remotely, unlovingly and impassively abiding somewhere in the heavenly spaces, watching the race which He created destroy itself.

2. THE DENIAL OF THE VIRGIN BIRTH AND INCARNATION IS TO DENY THAT THE LORD JESUS CHRIST

CAME INTO THE WORLD TO REVEAL THE IDEAL
HUMANITY.

Man, fallen, in his state of sin and guilt, has
never reached the ideal which God has established
and reserved for a redeemed society. It is impossible
for man to reach this goal by himself, by means of
his own capabilities and capacities. He cannot reach
even those ideals he has set for himself. Yet, in the
beginning man was made in the image and likeness
of God. That was God's intention and purpose and
that was man's destiny. How far man has fallen
short of that destiny is apparent to all. The depths
of human degradation and depravity are clear from
Romans 1:18-32; 3:9-18. But the ideal remains and
the destiny of redeemed man is revealed in Christ
incarnate. First John 3:2 (LT) says, "Beloved, now
we are children of God, and it does not yet appear what we shall be, but we know that when
He shall appear, *we shall be like Him,* for we shall
see Him as He is." In Christ, we shall finally attain
that destiny, we shall realize the great ideal and we
shall be like Christ Himself. Thus, in Christ we
shall at last bear the image and likeness of God.
In Him, we shall finally reach the grand and blessed
goal of true and perfect manhood, that manhood
God means us to reach, the likeness to God Himself.

Not yet, however, has God publicly manifested
the glory that belongs to His children in their
attainment of the ideal manhood. Not yet do we
appear as we shall be. But we still wrestle with the
flesh and struggle against the imperfections and

93

infirmities of the present physical body. In this sinful world, with our mortal nature, we wearily move on toward the goal that is certain. With the grace and strength of the Lord sustaining us and empowered by Him for service, we march onward, anticipating that glorious destiny which is ours in the wonderful plan of God. We have not yet realized the divine ideal: "But we see Jesus, who was made a little lower than the angels for the suffering of death, crowned with glory and honour..." (Heb. 2:9), and we are thus encouraged. If, however, it was not really in the flesh that Christ came or if it was not by virgin birth that He became incarnate in flesh, but was only the product of natural generation by two parents, then there is no such thing as an ideal humanity, there is no perfect manhood, there will be no new society of the redeemed. To deny Christ having come in flesh is thus to close the door to the realization of the "hope of glory." It is to deny the Head of the new race of redeemed humanity and the pledge of what we shall be, as set forth in the great passage, 1 Corinthians 15:45-49 (New Scofield):

> And so it is written, The first man, Adam, was made a living soul; the last Adam was made a life-giving spirit. However, that was not first which is spiritual, but that which is natural; and afterward that which is spiritual. The first man is of the earth, earthy; the second man is the Lord from heaven. As is the earthy, such are they also that are earthy; and as is the heavenly, such are they also that are heavenly. And as we have borne

94

the image of the earthy, we shall also bear the image of the heavenly.

The denial of this Scripture record, however, cannot overturn its truth. The facts stand as written. Adam began as the dust of earth, and God formed that dust into a body composed of earth. God breathed into it His breath and Adam became a living being, head of the human race. But the very opposite is true with regard to Christ. The person of the Son of God existed from all eternity, and by divine volition and power a human body was conceived in the virgin's womb, in which the person of the Son became incarnate. This was not merely for the purpose of His own existence in human flesh, but to redeem the fallen race, and to reveal what God has in store for a redeemed humanity. The image we now bear is an earthy one, derived from Adam. But the image we shall bear one day is heavenly, derived from our blessed and glorious Lord. What our bodies will be like and with what powers and functions they will be endowed when we meet the Lord, we cannot now fully describe. But we have before us the perfect model and example in our Lord Jesus Christ. In Him we have what we ought to be striving for even now. He is the ideal Man; His is the ideal humanity. And "...when He shall appear, we shall be like him" (1 John 3:2).

3. THE DENIAL OF THE VIRGIN BIRTH AND INCARNATION IS TO DENY THE SUPREME PURPOSE FOR WHICH CHRIST CAME INTO THE WORLD: TO BRING SALVA-

The Scriptures leave no doubt that the great purpose for Christ's coming in flesh was to die for sinners and thus save them from their sins. Death is primarily the separation of body and spirit. Hence, because God is pure spirit, He could not die. Therefore, He became flesh, taking true human nature, in order that He might die the atoning death on the cross. The writer of the Epistle to the Hebrews states: "We are sanctified through the offering *of the body* of Jesus Christ once for all" (10:10). The body, miraculously prepared by the power of the Holy Spirit in the womb of the virgin, became the substitutionary offering by the shedding of its blood, both body and blood thus becoming the expiatory sacrifice. Our Lord Jesus Christ Himself said to His apostles: "... the Son of Man came not to be ministered unto, but to minister, and *to give His life* a ransom for many" (Matt. 20:28). His life involved His flesh and blood—the price with which we have been bought (1 Cor. 6:20). The ransom of which He spoke was a payment by expiation: the payment of His life given unto death by sacrifice (1 Cor. 11:24) and shedding of His blood (Matt. 26:28; Luke 22:20). Hebrews 9:26 says that Christ "hath...appeared to put away sin *by the sacrifice of himself.*" And Peter testifies: "For Christ also hath once suffered for sins, the just for the unjust, that He might bring us to God, *being put to death in the flesh,* but made alive by

96

the Spirit" (1 Pet. 3:18, New Scofield). And Paul wrote to the Galatians: "But when the fulness of the time was come, God sent forth His Son, *made of a woman,* made under the law, to redeem them that were under the law" (Gal. 4:4-5a).

But it was not enough to die the sacrificial death of a substitute and to save men from their sins. Men are dead spiritually. They are without life. Hence, Christ came to share with men His own eternal life. He said to the multitudes who came to Capernaum seeking Him: "I am the living bread that came down from heaven; if any man eat of this bread, *he shall live forever;* and the bread that I will give is my flesh, which I will give *for the life* of the world" (John 6:51, New Scofield). And again He said, this time addressing the religious leaders of the day, "I am come that they *might have life,* and that they might have it more abundantly" (John 10:10). He is the mediator of life with all its abundant blessings, but He is more than this. He is the one and only source of existence and life for all the saved. In the person of the Son, God sent us "the life." He "became poor, that ye... might be rich" (2 Cor. 8:9). Jesus Christ having come in the flesh has enriched all of human life, and beyond that there is the unlimited richness of life He gives to all who know Him.

To deny that Jesus Christ became incarnate in flesh by means of the Virgin Birth, is to deny the Saviorhood of Christ and the impartation of life to men who are dead in their sins. If Jesus Christ is mere man and nothing more than the son of two human parents, even though He may be the flower of humanity as some modernists allow, His death could not save sinners from their sins and it would be impossible for Him to impart eternal life to men. Without the coming of the Lord of glory in flesh, there can be no atonement. If there is no atonement, then there can be no salvation and eternal life cannot be the possession of any man. Eternal life for sinners emanates from the cross of Christ. It comes to all those who eat the flesh of the Son of God by faith. Therefore He must become flesh, in order that His flesh may be given on the cross for the life of the world. The death of Christ at Calvary was required to make His life available to sinners. Through the matchless grace of God, we now may enter the holy place to come before God Himself "by a new and living way, which He hath consecrated for us, through the veil, that is to say, *His flesh...*" (Heb. 10:19, 20). The Son who came by virgin birth and incarnation for the suffering of death, the crucified Christ, is the entrance veil. Jesus said, "No man cometh unto the Father, but by Me" (John 14:6), that is by My flesh, My blood, by this veil. This veil shuts out and forever hides the Father and His family-home in heaven from all those who spurn it and deny it as the one and only means of entry. This theology fills not only the Epistle to the Hebrews, but all of the New Testament.

4. THE DENIAL OF THE VIRGIN BIRTH AND INCARNA-

TION IS TO DENY THAT BY THE COMING INTO THE
WORLD OF THE SON OF GOD, THE WORKS OF SATAN
HAVE BEEN OVERCOME.

First John 3:8 says: "...For this purpose the Son
of God was manifested, that He might destroy the
works of the devil." Hebrews 2:14 uses similar
language and applies the divine purpose to the
destruction of the Devil himself: "He [Christ] also
Himself likewise took part of the same [flesh and
blood]; that through death He might destroy him
that had the power of death, that is, the devil." In
certain respects, this purpose for Christ having
come in the flesh is the most significant of all. Our
Lord Jesus Christ was manifested to take away our
sins and to share with us His own eternal life. Yet
men are under the delusion and deception of Satan,
the prince of this age. Their minds and hearts are
beclouded and blinded by the satanic system of lies.
Men abide in Satan's realm which is well organized
indeed and which is the realm of death. Nothing
but the manifestation of the Son of God in the flesh
can deal adequately with this system, and overthrow
the Devil and his kingdom of darkness and death.
If the significant last clause of 1 John 3:8—"that
he might destroy the works of the devil"—is to be
properly rendered, and taken in agreement with the
context, then it must be understood to mean in
essence, that the Son of God was manifested to
overthrow what Satan has done and is doing. Christ
came in the flesh, to counteract and counterwork
the Devil, with regard to all of Satan's doings

(Greek *ta erga*), in general. But particularly was Christ's coming in flesh to undo the work of Satan who imparted to us the germ or seed of his own great sin of insubordination to and rebellion against the authority and Word of God. The Son of God was manifested to break up and destroy that work of sinning, which is the Devil's nature. The fall and ruin of the race began with wrong conceptions about God and disobedience to His commands. The Devil's lie was the source of the ruin; the revelation of the true God in flesh is the source of the remedy.

That such is the mind of John is clear from verse 8. He states: "He that committeth sin is of the devil; for the devil sinneth from the beginning" (v. 8a). Literally the first clause reads: "The one doing the sin is from the devil...." The Devil is the father of all who keep on doing sin (John 8:44); they are all "the children of the devil." This is a fatherhood which is due to the derivation of our sinning from the Devil's sinning, "because from the beginning, the Devil sins," that is, the progressive present tense of the verb "sin" gathers up past and present sinning into one expression: "sins and keeps on sinning." All who follow him in the sinning, and themselves keep on in the sin are "his children." Let us not be deceived in this matter (v. 7). Let no one think that Satan is not real and his designs and devices of little consequence. We are either in the family of God, having been declared righteous (v. 7), or we are members of the Devil's family, under condemnation, and do not know God (v. 6, 10; Eph. 2:1-3).

The overthrow of Satan and the dissolution of his works, is next specifically stated by John as the particular purpose of Christ's coming in the flesh: "For this the Son of God was manifested, that He might destroy the works of the devil." We are not to think of "destroy" as meaning annihilation or total destruction which leaves no traces in its wake. The verb is here to be taken as meaning: "overthrow," in the sense of breaking up something that was compactly built together, depriving it of authority and effectiveness, while undoing its achievements. It would thus mean to loose those who were bound by it. In this sense, the Devil and his works were "destroyed." We know that these have not been destroyed in the absolute sense. But we have been released from Satan's rule, his control, and his works which were like chains that bound us tightly. Now he and his works have been deprived of their force and authority, they have been overthrown, rendered inoperative and ineffective. The Devil is still active, and engaged in carrying out his evil works, but he has been defeated by Christ's coming in the flesh, and in Him we have victory and freedom from the Devil's tyranny.

The aorist tense of the verb "destroy" shows how definitely and effectively the Lord was to perform the work of destruction. He came to break up decisively the havoc which Satan wrought among men by his sinning. This was done supremely through the atoning death and physical resurrection of the Lord Jesus Christ. By this, the destiny of the arch-enemy of God was sealed. But not by this alone did the Lord destroy the Devil's works. "The Son of God *was manifested....*" By His coming down from heaven, and *appearing in the flesh*, He destroyed the works of the Devil and his power of deception and death. There is something to be seen in this, which is unusually significant, and which Robert S. Candlish notes in his commentary on 1 John 3:8.

In thus destroying the works of the devil, in this sense and to this effect, His being manifested as the Son of God was, in itself alone, a great step. For He was manifested in the very form, in the very position, which the devil had himself felt, and had persuaded us to feel, to be grievous, irksome, and intolerable. He, being the Son, "took upon Him the form of a servant." He was so manifested as to make it plain beyond all question, that there is no such root of bitterness as the devil would insinuate that there is, in a creature's subjection as a servant to the law of God His Creator, in the Son's subjection as a servant to the law of God His Father. The Son of God is manifested as submitting to that place of subordination to authority which the devil and his angels spurned; giving Himself to a service infinitely more humiliating than they were called to when they were commanded to worship Him."[1]

1 Robert S. Candlish, *The First Epistle of John,* (Grand Rapids, Michigan: The Zondervan Publishing House, 1940) , p. 287.

This was a death blow to the works of the Devil. It destroyed at the very roots, the staple and substance of His power. When the Son of God was manifested in flesh, and demonstrated to all the world that it was no degradation or bondage for the Son Himself to be the humble servant of the Father, it destroyed the Devil's works. The Son took the form of a slave and was made in the likeness of men; yet He lived apart from sin, never acting independently of His relationship with the Father. In this was seen the very proof and perfection of His person through which He destroyed the works of the Devil. And when in the form of a servant, as the Man miraculously conceived in the womb of the virgin, He successfully met and defeated the dreadful onslaught of Satan in the great temptation, He destroyed the Devil's works. The Son of God could be tempted (tested) because He became man. He alone of the three great persons of the Holy Trinity, by assuming our nature, could suffer human hunger, and could be challenged to appease that hunger in a sinful way. He alone, by His human nature, was dependent upon His heavenly Father, and could thus be asked to abuse this dependence by a false trust in His Father. He alone, in His human nature, having come in the flesh, faced the cross and could be tempted to evade it and pursue another course. Such temptation was possible only with respect to the humanity of the Lord.

At the same time it was *because of* the miraculous

conception and birth of the Lord of glory into the world that He could resist the tempter and smite him with defeat. For He was the pre-existent Son of God, and could enter the realm of human life *only by supernatural means*. Hence, because He was not merely *a* son of God, but *the* Son of God, the second Person of the great Godhead incarnate, *He could not fall into sin*. Jesus Christ, the Lord from Heaven, remained unmoved under all the forces Satan could hurl against Him, because He was the eternal God manifest in the flesh to destroy the works of the Devil. Thus to deny Christ's having come in the flesh is to deny that the works of the Devil have been overthrown, that the great adversary has been judged (John 16:11), and that believers are kept and guarded from his powers and influences (John 17:15, 20; 1 John 5:18). It is to deny that the Devil is overcome and defeated by the power of Christ and by His Word (1 John 2:13, 14; 4:4). If Christ was not manifested in flesh by virgin birth, then His Word is unreliable, the Devil's works continue unchecked and unjudged, the Devil himself is not actually under divine sentence and he may do with us as he pleases.

Presently, the Devil's ultimate overthrow has not yet been carried out by Christ. Satan is still allowed his headship of the age and the exercise of his wily schemes and designs. His activity is described by Peter as that of "walking about, seeking whom he may devour" (1 Pet. 5:8). This manner of expression by Peter portrays the danger, and stresses the need for sobriety and vigilance on the part of true Christians toward the Devil and his work. Believers however, are now preserved from Satan's deadly expert methods by the full armor of God, and are standing against the Devil with that armor ever in use (Eph. 6:11-18). The destruction of the Devil's works began effectively and decisively when the Son of God was manifested in the flesh; it is moving forward to its inevitable and inexorable consummation, already divinely decreed (cf. Rev. 20:1-3; 20:7-10).

5. THE DENIAL OF THE VIRGIN BIRTH AND INCARNATION IS TO DENY THE PRESENT GREAT HIGH PRIESTLY MINISTRY OF THE LORD JESUS CHRIST.

Hebrews 2:17 testifies: "Hence He [Christ] was obliged in all things *to be made like His brethren* in order to be merciful and a faithful High Priest as to the things pertaining to God, for the purpose of expiating the sins of the people" (LT). Since the Son of God was bound in all respects to be like His brothers in the flesh, He too must take for Himself human flesh, form and nature. Even the eternal almighty God, with all His omnipotence and omniscience, could not know human life by experience without entering human life and living it. He came down and entered into our life in order that He might know by actual experience the problems of human existence. He needed the experience of human life, so that He might be for us a merciful High Priest, a compassionate and sympathetic Savior. Although He was previously compassionate, for actually His great mercy and compassion dictated His coming in human flesh by virgin birth, yet He must have the experience of *human* compassion, so essential to the High Priest who ministers for His brethren in the flesh. He must know our infirmities and temptations (Heb. 4:14, 15); to bring men to God, He must be a man ministering in behalf of men (1 Tim. 2:5).

Since "we have a great High Priest, having gone through the heavens, Jesus, the Son of God, let us continue to hold fast the confession" (Heb. 4:14 —LT). How this reminds us of 1 John 4:2 which says, "...every spirit who confesses Jesus Christ having come in flesh is from God" (LT). Having *Him,* let us keep holding fast what we know to be true about Him. We have the greatest, strongest incentive for holding fast this confession of Him. We have a High Priest Who came down from Heaven, and assuming our nature but without sin, wrought salvation for sinners. Now, having risen from the dead and passed through the heavens, beyond the limitations of the created universe, into the absolute presence of God, Jesus Christ sits as equal with God, interceding and availing for us. "Jesus, the Son of God" expresses both His natures: "Jesus" marking His true humanity, and "Son of God" denoting His deity. The first designates the essential condition of His *being* our High Priest; the second shows that His High Priesthood *is avail-ing.* As "Jesus," He became lower than the angels, and was born of the virgin, becoming incarnate, in order that He might "taste death for every man" (Heb. 2:9). As "Son of God," He was exalted infinitely above the angels, and ascended back to the glory He had enjoyed with the Father, ". . . now to appear in the presence of God for us" (Heb. 9:24).

How great, and how completely necessary, is His ministry as our High Priest! Our infirmities, frailties, and weaknesses have a tendency to dispose us toward neglecting our confession, instead of holding to it with tenacity and strength. But here is the answer that encourages us, and helps us to overcome the weaknesses: "For we do not have a High Priest not able to be sympathetic with our weaknesses. . ." (Heb. 4:15a—LT). The negative manner of expression is much more forceful because it is more full and formal than a simple affirmative. It better contrasts the dreadful alternative; that is, of having a High Priest who cannot, or will not, be sympathetic with our infirmities or of having no High Priest at all. This indeed is the fact, if Christ did not come in the flesh by virgin birth, and thus He did not die on the cross and rise from the dead. But the very contrary is true: we *do have* a High Priest who knows all our weaknesses from His own human experience, and Who is thus able to be sympathetic with us in our infirmities and trials. For He was tried in all respects in like manner (as we), except for sin. His personal name "Jesus" is the name of His humiliation which He bore here on the earth when He took upon Himself our human weaknesses. How then, could we possibly think that the Lord does not feel and sympathize with us (*sumpascho*), in our weaknesses and frailties? "For in that He has suffered, He Himself, having come to be tempted, is able to help those who are tempted" (Heb. 2:18—LT).

This verse (Heb. 2:18) presents a unique study in verb tenses. The perfect tense "He has suffered" (*peponthen*) indicates and includes the whole duration of the Lord's suffering which finally was terminated by His death on the cross. The aorist participle which follows: "He Himself, having been tempted" (*autos peirastheis*), points to the past fact that our Lord Jesus Christ was definitely tempted, and connects this fact with His suffering. We may think of His dreadful beatings in the praetorium, or of Gethsemane where He wrestled in prayer. The present tense "is able" (*dunatai*), means that He is ever and always able, enduringly so, to succor us. There is never even a single point of time when He is not able to do so. The present participle "those who are tempted" (*tois peiradzomenois*), refers to people of God, who, time after time, experience temptings. Human life is marked by suffering and temptation. But just as we are required to face the bitter trials of earthly living, we must also remember that Christ continues able to deliver us. The final verbal expression, the infinitive "to help" (*boeitheisai*), is the effective aorist: our blessed Lord is definitely able to actually and conclusively help us. There is absolutely no doubt in the punctiliar action. He *is* able to help, to rescue, to deliver, to succor us. For, having suffered as He did, having been tempted as He was, there can be no doubt that He can help all His own, whose lot it is to now and throughout life on earth to experience suffering and temptation. This entire statement in Hebrews 2:18 attests the fact that the Lord endured the suffering triumphantly, and conquered the temptation. At the beginning of His ministry, Jesus met the indescribably dreadful assault of Satan in its every aspect, with the words of Holy Scripture. As His work was drawing to its climax and conclusion, He faced the temptation to evade the awful suffering and death on the cross, with His words to the Father: "Not My will be done, but Thine!" Then He placed Himself into the hands of His enemies (John 18:4-12).

Having such a great High Priest, then "let us therefore keep approaching the throne of the grace with boldness, in order that we may obtain mercy and find grace for timely need" (Heb. 4:16—LT). How could this be possible if our High Priest is not the pre-existent Son of God, virgin-born into human flesh? Only if He is supernatural can He occupy the place of authority, power and mediatorship, at God's right hand. It would be ridiculous indeed to contend that an ordinary man has been conveyed up into Heaven, in order that he might act as a High Priest for us. Such a thing is not only inane, but impossible. Yet it is not more so than to deny that our great High Priest, presently at the throne of God, did not enter the world in the flesh by virgin birth. If the non-confessors of this fundamental of the faith are right in their denial and rejection of this basic truth, then there is no such High Priest in Heaven interceding for us, presenting the merit of His blood in behalf of true Christians, mercifully mediating our communication with our Heavenly Father. He has induced us to take a path which we cannot follow, and which contrary to all our expectations, does not lead to the source of mercy and grace. To deny the Son of God having come in the flesh is to deny both *the person* of the great High Priest, and *the place* of His high priestly ministry. It is to relegate Him to the order of priests in Old Testament times. It is to make Him no better than they whose ministry, one after the other, was stopped by death. "But He on account of His remaining forever, hath an unchangeable priesthood; whence also He is able to save to the utmost those who come through Him to God, ever living to make intercession for them" (Heb. 7:24, 25—LT). The present tenses in these two verses: "continueth" (*menein*), "hath" (*echei*), "is able" (*dunatai*), "liveth" (*dzon*) and "make intercession" (*entugchanein*), bring out the important characteristic of the Lord's priestly work. He is really there in God's presence, living, ever continuing to intercede in behalf of us. And the intercessory work of Christ cannot be separated from His supernatural entrance into human existence and His priestly life, death, resurrection and exaltation.

As Lenski aptly said:

> The right conception is that He bases all His intercession on this other work. It is correct to say, that in interceding, He makes His whole mediatorial work count for our benefit with God.[1]

6. THE DENIAL OF THE VIRGIN BIRTH AND INCARNATION IS TO DENY THE POSSIBILITY OF REAL COMMUNION BETWEEN GOD AND MAN.

To deny that there can be any real union between the divine and the human, between God and man, is one of the worst aspects of unbelief. Christ having come in flesh by virgin birth manifests the dignity and sacredness of human life and is the answer to all the religious and philosophical errors concerning the physical existence. Contrary to the view that the physical life is something vile and mean, and not worth having, human life *is* worthwhile, so much so that the Son of God could enter into it. The fall has degraded physical life and given to mankind a depraved nature. Yet the Son of God, having come in the flesh, lived as Man without sin. He proved that sin is not an essential quality of the physical life and that physical life did not contaminate and corrupt His purity. Thus He "condemned sin in the flesh" (Rom. 8:3). The fact of Jesus Christ having come in the flesh satis-

---

1 R.C.H. Lenski, *Interpretation of the Epistle to the Hebrews*, (Columbus, Ohio: Lutheran Book Concern, 1938), pp. 240-241.

fies the longing of men for a mediator with God who is truly human. Job 9:33 expresses this need, "Neither is there any daysman [mediator] between us, that might lay his hand upon us both" (New Scofield). In the middle ages, when the deity and true humanity of Christ were ignored, perverted, or explained away, men turned to angels, the virgin Mary, and to saints, revealing the yearning of the human heart for someone human to mediate and intercede. The answer for this is the virgin-born, incarnate Savior, the God-Man.

All the difficulties and problems surrounding the mystery of the person of Christ will never be solved. The great difficulty is that of understanding how the Lord could have but one personality when He possessed two real natures, divine and human. How can these natures be united in the one Person? This is the "mystery of godliness" (1 Tim. 3:16). But the Bible is clear in its testimony. The Lord always spoke of Himself as *one personality,* not two (John 8:18, 23; 16:7). It is important to note that He never distinguished Himself as a divine person from Himself as a true human being: that is, He never severed the two natures. In John 8:58, the Savior born of Mary speaks and says: "Before Abraham was, *I am.*" He does not say: "Before Abraham was, My divine nature existed." There are many evidences of the two natures in the one Person, appearing side by side, in the Scriptures. This problem was discussed and debated at great length during the Council of Chalcedon in 451 A.D., and a remarkable creed was drawn up, which carefully guarded against error:

> He is one Christ, existing in two natures without mixture, without division, without separation; the diversity of the natures not being destroyed by their union in the one person; but the peculiar properties of each nature being preserved and concurring to the one person.

The coming of Christ in the flesh establishes the fact that there is no unbridgeable gap between God and human nature. For in Christ the divine and human natures are united in one person. The unbridgeable antagonism is not between God and human nature, but between God and fallen, sinful human nature. The great mystery of Christ's person cannot be exhaustively studied, explored, or described, and it assuredly teaches intellectual humility to Christian teachers and preachers. There are some matters that are beyond us, which we shall never totally comprehend. After we have exercised all our capacities, and have searched the extremities of our minds under the illumination of the Holy Spirit of God, we must finally fall upon our faces before the mystery of the eternal, almighty God in Christ, having come in flesh, and confess that we cannot explain Him. But thank God everlastingly *that we know Him*. We must also thank God that the great practical value of Christ's Incarnation by Virgin Birth is that in this present time, during these days of earthly experience, we may be blessed with real communion and communication with the

God of Heaven. Let us be assured that we are not dealing with a far-off deity who sits in the heavenly splendor, impassively watching us struggle along in the difficulties and agonies of human life, with no way to reach that God. We belong to One who was willing to come down from heaven, enter into human life, and thus to know that life by personal experience. For that purpose, He was manifested; the Word became flesh. "And we know that the Son of God has come, and hath given us an understanding in order that we may know the true One..." (1 John 5:20). Our fellowship and communion are with Him. This is the true God and eternal life.

7. The denial of the Virgin Birth and Incarnation is to deny that Christ is the final and impartial Judge of all men.

The deniers of the doctrine of Christ will one day face the very One whose supernatural person and power they have denied. They will be among the multitudes of unbelievers, many of whom will be religious, who stand before the Judge of all men (2 Tim. 4:1; Rev. 19:16). "For the Father judgeth no man, but hath committed all judgment unto the Son" (John 5:22). Again, John records that the Father "hath given Him [the Son] authority to execute judgment also, *because He is the Son of Man*" (John 5:27). The verb in each instance is the same. In verse 22 it is the perfect tense, *dedoka* (hath committed, KJV) and in verse 27 it is the aorist tense, *edoka* (hath given, KJV). In verse 22, the perfect form contains a veiled reference to the Incarnation by the Virgin Birth of the Son. The fact that the words "hath committed" refer to the human nature of the Son is then fully brought out in verse 27. The Father has given to the Son the authority to execute judgment "because He is the Son of Man." It is because He humbled Himself to take human flesh, form and nature, and to be born of the virgin, that He will be the One to execute judgment upon all mankind. Dean Burgon once said: "Because of His alliance with man's nature, because of His sense of man's infirmities, because of all He did for man's sake as the Son of Man, the Son is that person of the Trinity who is most fit, as well as most worthy, to be man's Judge." It is true that the Virgin Birth is not here specifically designated, because the term "man" (*anthropos*) might refer to either sex. Still, it *is* predicated because the Lord used this word only with reference to His mother, Mary—not as concerning two parents, mother and father. He here states that, as a gift from the Heavenly Father sent into the world through the portal of the Virgin Birth, He can and does receive the right and power (*exousia*) to act as the Judge of all men. He could only receive this gift for His human nature, which is emphasized by the absence of the definite article before the noun, "Son." It is not *The* Son of Man, but simply *Son of Man,* indicating character and quality, and thus emphasizing the human nature of Christ. The Son

entered the world by being born man (John 1:14),
the son of a human being (Mary), incarnate in
human flesh by miraculous birth (John 1:26-38;
2:6, 7). No other "Son of Man" could even become
the recipient of such authority as this—to act as
sovereign Judge of all mankind. To deny this is
thus to deny that the Lord was virgin-born; it is to
deny that God has appointed a day "in the which
He will judge the world in righteousness by that
Man whom He hath ordained..." (Acts 17:31). It
is to deny that the Savior, having first come in the
flesh, will sit in judgment of men and nations at
His return. It is to erroneously insist instead that
God will, in the end, approve a universalistic salvation of all men, irrespective of their sins. This latter
idea is the popular theological view in our day,
and is taught by many religious leaders whose theology is liberal and unbiblical. They do not confess
true belief in the doctrine of Christ and disparage
particularly the Virgin Birth and Incarnation.
Their unbelief concerning the supernatural entrance of the Lord Jesus Christ into human life
dictates their refusal to accept Him as the final
Judge of all men.

Contrary to all the false teachings and Satanic
deceptions which characterize the liberal theology
of our day, all men will not be saved at the end,
but all unsaved men *will stand* in the presence of
the great Judge of all the world in the final day
of reckoning. All is not over when men die.
Whether they like it or not, irrespective of who

they are and how many good works they will claim to have done in the Lord's name, they will have to come forth from their graves at the last day and face the Lord of glory at the White Throne judgment. Not one can escape His summons, for it is the command of God. When His voice penetrates the graves of the world and calls men out of them, and before Him, all must obey. Our blessed Lord will judge all men fairly, justly, and impartially— but judgment *there will be*. The words of Christ are plain and unmistakable. Thus it is written, and thus it must be.

The saints, on the other hand, have been delivered from penal judgment, and will not come under the wrath of God (John 5:24; 1 Thess. 1:10; 5:9). They wait expectantly for the moment when the Lord Himself "shall descend from heaven with a shout, with the voice of the archangel, and with the trump of God: and the dead in Christ shall rise first: Then we which are alive and remain shall be caught up together with them in the clouds, to meet the Lord in the air: and so shall we ever be with the Lord" (1 Thess. 4:16-17). He is our total hope, and His appearing is our blessed hope. "And every man that hath this hope in him purifieth himself, even as He is pure" (1 John 3:3). Let us be sure that we see the great practical significance of this statement. It is the essential purity of the Lord's truly human nature set before us here. The lesson for us is this: as we wait for the Lord to come for us, we are drawn to Him even now. The binding responsibility of purifying ourselves is laid upon us in such a world-age, evil and unfavorably disposed toward us, as it was toward Him and His purity. His being pure in such hateful circumstances is then the great incentive for our obediently and consistently purifying ourselves. The world-age hated Him for this, it will hate us too for being like Him. Nevertheless while the whole age lies in the power of the wicked one and in this age we have tribulation, let us be of good cheer, for the Lord of glory has overcome the world. Even so, come, Lord Jesus!

Bibliography

Aglen, A. "The Song of Solomon," *Ellicott's Commentary,* (Grand Rapids: Zondervan Publishing House, 1954), Vol. IV.

Alexander, J. A. *The Psalms,* (New York: Chas. Scribner & Co., 1871), Vols. I & II.

_____ *Commentary on the Prophecies of Isaiah,* (Grand Rapids: Zondervan Publishing House, 1953).

Alford, Henry. "The Gospel According to Matthew," *The Greek Testament,* (London: Rivingtons, 1863), Vol. I.

_____ "The Gospel According to Luke," *The Greek Testament,* (London: Rivingtons, 1863), Vol. I.

_____ "The Epistle of St. John," *The Greek Testament,* (London: Rivingtons, 1862), Vol. IV.

Anderson, Sir Robert. *The Lord From Heaven,* (Wheaton: Van Kampen Press, n.d.).

Ball, C. J. "First Chronicles," *Ellicott's Commentary,* (Grand Rapids: Zondervan Publishing House, 1954), Vol. III.

Barclay, William. "First John," *The Letters of John and*

Jude, (Philadelphia: The Westminster Press, 1958).

Bertram, R. A. *A Homiletical Commentary on the Prophecies of Isaiah,* (New York: Funk & Wagnalls Co., 1892), Vol. I.

Bloomfield, S. T. *The Greek Testament with English Notes,* (Philadelphia: Clark and Hesser, 1854), Vol. I.

Broadus, John A. "The Gospel of Matthew," *American Commentary on the New Testament,* (Philadelphia: The American Baptist Publication Society, 1886), Vol. I.

Bruce, A. B. *The Humiliation of Christ,* (Grand Rapids: Wm. B. Eerdmans Publishing Co., 1955).

_____ "The Gospel of Matthew," *The Expositor's Greek Testament,* (Grand Rapids: Wm. B. Eerdmans, Publishing Co., n.d.).

_____ "The Gospel of Luke," *The Expositor's Greek Testament,* (Grand Rapids: Wm. B. Eerdmans Publishing Co., n.d.).

Candlish, Robert S. *The First Epistle of John,* (Grand Rapids: Zondervan Publishing House, 1940).

Deane, W. J. "The Proverbs," *The Pulpit Commentary,* (New York: Funk & Wagnalls Company, 1944).

Exell, J. S. *A Homiletical Commentary on the Book of Exodus,* (New York: Funk & Wagnalls Company, 1892).

Green, Dr. "The Song of Solomon," *Lange's Commentary,* (Grand Rapids: Zondervan Publishing House, n.d.).

Green, Samuel G. *A Handbook to the Grammar of the Greek Testament,* (New York: Fleming H. Revell Company, n.d.).

Holdsworth, W. W. *The Christ of the Gospels,* (New York: Eaton & Mains, 1911).

Jacobus, M. W. "Notes on the Gospels," *Matthew and Mark*, (New York: Robert Carter & Brothers, 1873).

Lenski, R. C. H. *The Interpretation of St. Matthew's Gospel*, (Columbus: The Wartburg Press, 1943).

_____ *The Interpretation of St. Mark's and St. Luke's Gospels*, (Columbus: The Lutheran Book Concern, 1934).

_____ *The Interpretation of the Epistle to the Hebrews*, (Columbus: The Lutheran Book Concern, 1938).

Leupold, H. C. *Exposition of Genesis*, (Columbus, The Wartburg Press, 1942).

Machen, J. Gresham. *The Virgin Birth of Christ*, (New York: Harper & Brothers Publishers, 1930).

Meyer, H. A. W. *Critical and Exegetical Handbook to the Gospel of Matthew*, (New York: Funk & Wagnalls Publishers, 1884).

_____ *Critical and Exegetical Handbook to the Gospels of Mark and Luke*, (New York: Funk & Wagnalls Publishers, 1884).

McClain, Alva J. *The Virgin Birth in the RSV* (The Brethren Missionary Herald, Feb. 28, 1953).

_____ *Unpublished Notes in Systematic Theology*, Grace Theological Seminary, 1943.

Morgan, G. Campbell. *The Crises of the Christ*, (New York: Fleming H. Revell Company, 1936).

Naegelsbach, Dr. "The Prophet Isaiah," *Lange's Commentary*, (Grand Rapids: Zondervan Publishing House, n.d.).

Nutt, J. W. "The Proverbs," *Ellicott's Commentary*, (Grand Rapids: Zondervan Publishing House, n.d.), Vol. IV.

Orr, James. "The Virgin Birth of Christ," *The Funda-*

mentals, (The Bible Institute of Los Angeles, 1917),
Vol. II.

Perowne, J. J. Stewart. *The Book of Psalms,* (Grand
Rapids: Zondervan Publishing House, 1960), Vols.
I, II.

Rawlinson, George. "The Book of Exodus," *Ellicott's
Commentary,* (Grand Rapids: Zondervan Publishing
House, 1954), Vol. I.

Schneider, Johannes. *Jesus Christ: His Life and Ministry,*
(Calwer Bibellexikon, published in 1960 by Calwer
Verlag in Stuttgart).

Simpson, P. C. *The Fact of Christ,* (New York: Fleming
H. Revell Co., 1900).

Smith, R. P. "The Book of Genesis," *Ellicott's Commentary,* (Grand Rapids: Zondervan Publishing House,
1954), Vol. I.

Stock, John. "The God-Man," *The Fundamentals,* (The
Bible Institute of Los Angeles, 1917), Vol. II.

Strong, A. H. *Systematic Theology,* (Philadelphia: The
Judson Press, 1907).

Sweet, Louis M. "The Virgin Birth of Jesus Christ," *The
International Bible Encyclopedia,* (Grand Rapids:
Wm. B. Eerdmans Publishing Co., 1939), Vol. V.

Trinitarian Bible Society *Quarterly Record,* April-June
Issue, 1970.

Vincent, Marvin R. "The Gospel According to Matthew,"
Word Studies in the New Testament, (Grand Rapids:
Wm. B. Eerdmans Publishing Co., 1946), Vol. I.

Vine, W. E. *Isaiah,* (London: Oliphants Limited, 1953).

Wolfendale, James. *A Homiletical Commentary on the
Book of First Chronicles,* (New York: Funk &
Wagnalls Co., 1892).

Zockler, Otto. "The Proverbs," *Lange's Commentary,* (Grand Rapids: Zondervan Publishing House, n.d.).

GREEK TESTAMENTS

Nestle, E. *Hei Kainei Diatheikei,* (London: The British and Foreign Bible Society, 1939).

Souter, A. *Novum Testamentum Graece,* (Oxonii, Excudebat Horatius Hart, Typographus academicus).

Westcott, B. F., and Hort, F. J. A. *The New Testament in the Original Greek,* (New York: The MacMillan Company, 1940).

OLD TESTAMENT TEXTS

Kittle, R. *Biblia Hebraica,* (For the American Bible Society, New York, published by Privileg. Wurtt. Bibelanstalt, Stuttgart).

Rosenthal, Franz. *A Grammar of Biblical Aramaic,* (Wiesbaden: Otto Harrassowitz, 1961).

GREEK LEXICONS

Arndt, W. F., and Gingrich, F. W. *A Greek-English Lexicon of the New Testament,* (Chicago: The University of Chicago Press, 1952).

Liddell, H. G., and Scott, Robert. *A Greek-English Lexicon,* (New York: Harper & Brothers Publishers, 1870).

Moulton, J. H., and Milligan, George. *The Vocabulary of the Greek Testament,* (Grand Rapids: Wm. B. Eerdmans Publishing Company, 1960).

Thayer, J. H. *A Greek-English Lexicon of the New Testament,* (New York: The American Book Company, and Harper & Brothers, 1886).

HEBREW LEXICONS

Harkavy, A. *Student's Hebrew-Chaldee Dictionary,* (Hebrew Publishing Co., no frontispiece).

Pick, Aaron. *The English and Hebrew Bible Student's Concordance,* (University of Prague: Bible Study Classic).

VERSIONS

Authorized Version, The. *The New Scofield Reference Bible,* (New York: The Oxford University Press, 1967).

Septuagint Version, The. *Edidit Alfred Rahlfs,* (For the American Bible Society, New York, published by Privileg. Wurtt. Bibelanstalt, Stuttgart, 1952).